SAFE & SOUND

A Proven Methodology for Protecting the Wealthy

RUSS ALAN PRINCE
PAUL MICHAEL VIOLLIS Sr., Ph.D.
ASA BRET PRINCE

5081 Olympic Boulevard
Erlanger, KY 41018
859.692.2100
www.NUCO.com

The National Underwriter Company
A Unit of Highline Media LLC

THE NATIONAL UNDERWRITER COMPANY
P.O. Box 14367
Cincinnati, OH 45250-0874

International Standard Book Number: 0-87218-715-2

Printed in The United States of America

DEDICATIONS:

To Jerry

- *Russ*

To Karen, Jennifer and Paul Michael...The core of my identity

- *Paul*

To my best friend Jerry

- *Ace*

About the Authors

Russ Alan Prince

Mr. Russ Prince is President of Prince & Associates, Inc., a research and consulting firm focused on the affluent market. He is one of the leading authorities on the private wealth industry and an internationally recognized expert on wealth protection strategies.

Paul Michael Viollis Sr., Ph.D.

Dr. Paul Viollis is President of Risk Control Strategies. Dr. Viollis is one of the foremost experts in providing security solutions to the wealthy. He has appeared and been quoted in media outlets including CNN, FOX NEWS, MSNBC, CNBC, CBS and more.

Asa Bret Prince

Mr. Asa Prince is a niche expert in the field of property protection strategies. He is regularly called upon to implement and oversee the security systems of some of the largest estates in North America.

Safe & Sound

A Proven Methodology for Protecting the Wealthy

FOREWORD

For the less than one percent of one percent of the world's populace that is deemed ultra-affluent, there are many ironies that are unique to this demographic. In today's uncertain world, affluence yields power, yet it is inherently vulnerable. It grants freedom but it also isolates. It generates financial security, but it is no longer the confidence of personal safety.

We are reminded in the morning paper and on the nightly news that the risks of living in this world are compounding year by year, and those risks are dramatically exacerbated for high-net-worth individuals. They have earned a level of affluence that requires them to pay a price for guarding their most important assets--human, financial and physical.

Whereas the rest of the world may view ultra affluence as a protected and secure society, Paul Viollis knows otherwise. He, Russ Alan Prince and Asa Bret Prince, have delivered in this book what is virtually a holistic insurance policy for optimal living with extreme wealth. In the pages that follow, they have re-engineered the culture of thinking of high net-worth families, and then devised a broad spectrum of security solutions that engages every facet of one's lifestyle—from personal identity, financial and legal concerns, to travel, education and family.

As conveyed in this book, a strategic vision weaves together disciplines and a score of consultants—an attorney, a legal advisor, personal/executive protection experts, and many other professional consultants. Expressed with clear insight and useful information, I think of this book as the "coming together" of divergent interests that may otherwise work against each other in support of the common security goals of an uncommonly wealthy party. For the ultra-affluent, this book can be an extraordinary compass to re-calibrate and navigate one's life.

Ultimately, a comprehensive approach to safety and security provides the gift of well-being and confidence. The act of guarding and protecting, if done right, can be truly liberating. It is an opportunity to be less afraid and self-assured, and more equipped with "the right resources and the right people, do the right things at the right time." Paul Viollis' philosophy is certainly an appealing alternative to living with chronic anxiety about physical security.

In turn, this perspective illuminates a different kind of methodology—the assessment, development and implementation of security *solutions*—that advocates a long-term view, one that can be modified as personal needs and external factors change.

As one of the veteran executives with The Breakers Palm Beach, one of America's legendary resort destinations, I and my colleagues are well familiar with the ultra-affluent market. Founded in 1896 by railroad magnate Henry Flagler, our luxury oceanfront destination has a longstanding history with this community. The Breakers has been a social hub on the island of Palm Beach, and serves as a primary vacation address for the wealthy, as their home away from home. We live in their universe every day.

While hosting the most discerning travelers from around the world as well as serving an exclusive club membership, The Breakers is also one of the region's leading employers. We have worked closely with Paul Viollis to enhance our capacities for safe-guarding our work environment for almost 2,000 staff members, while continually striving to enhance the guest experience. In that vein, risk control strategies that help foster employee and customer fulfillment have become very meaningful to our organization.

The Breakers Palm Beach is one of the few privately-held hotels in the US to remain independent of chain affiliation, and our entrepreneurial spirit inclines us to always stay ahead of emerging trends and organizational needs. We wholly subscribe to Paul's non-traditional thought process regarding safety and security, his critical way of thinking, and his sense of appropriateness. Our resort organization, like you, desires to control our destiny and achieve long-term security and success. We invite you to do the same under the guidance of Paul Viollis.

—Atesh Chandra, Vice President-Administration, The Breakers Palm Beach

How to Use This Book

Case Study #1

Lisa is a little taller than three feet. She has piercing blue eyes, a gift from her father. Her hair is the color of white gold, a gift from her mother.

Lisa, while very fond of pink ice cream says that her favorite food is pizza. She loves to ride horses and talks about owning and riding a hundred horses when she becomes a grownup. Lisa has an entire collection of Barbie dolls which she dutifully updates at FAO Schwarz. She likes going to kindergarten but says that she had more fun at preschool–her friends were nicer there.

At the age of six, Lisa disappeared. She was with her nanny of eight months when both of them did not come back from a play date in Central Park, New York City. Her parents tried unsuccessfully to contact the nanny by calling the cell phone they gave her. With no response after two hours of trying, they started to panic and called the police.

The family did not hear anything for about a month and then they received a note saying that Lisa was alright and that they would be in touch. Luckily, a week later a neighbor spotted a person that sort-of resembled the nanny. The police were contacted and they investigated.

It was the nanny, living with Lisa and her boyfriend. The nanny and her boyfriend was arrested and charged with kidnapping. The nanny had, according to Lisa's mother, impeccable credentials. She had previously worked for two years for a close friend of Lisa's mother. She went to top private schools and graduated from one of the best colleges in the United States. She had beautiful manners and Lisa adored her.

Before hiring the nanny, the family never conducted a formal background investigation. The investigation by the police once the nanny and her boyfriend were apprehended, turned up a gambling habit that had produced a $200,000 debt. The nanny thought she could erase her debt as well as make a profit by having her boyfriend "kidnap" her and Lisa and ransom them back to Lisa's family.

Case Study #2

After six years of playing parts in dramas and sitcoms on television and four big screen movies, with the last one being a blockbuster, his career took off. Now he is repeatedly offered very nice parts in television shows as well as solid roles in the movies.

While he is confident he will never be a big box office draw–a headliner–financially he is doing quite well. In the last few years, for example, he purchased a house in California and another one in Florida as well as a condominium in mid-town New York City. For all these purchases, he paid cash because he is anxious that the bottom will fall out of his career at any time.

Even as he was working to become a successful actor, it was extremely important to him to have personal time. He wants to keep some aspects of his life for himself and his family. He readily recognizes the need for good publicity, but he is adamant about keeping his family out of the limelight. His family's privacy became ever more important to him when he found out his twin four year old daughters had a rare but treatable genetic blood disease.

He became extremely upset when the paparazzi started to hound his family. Getting pictures of the twins as well as the distraught parents was worth serious money. He initially tried ducking all photographers when he was with his family. This avoidance strategy did not work in the slightest.

He hired a security consultant to come up with a way of protecting his family's privacy. The security consultant worked hard at altering the family's travel routes, but this approach also proved ineffective, and for a very good reason. It turned out that the actor's personal assistant was, for a fee, providing the paparazzi his family's itinerary. Carefully firing the personal assistant coupled with continuing to varying the routes has resulted in the privacy for his family he desired.

Case Study #3

It's a 26,000 square foot house sitting on nearly 50 acres. Included in the house is an indoor/outdoor swimming pool (the connection between the indoor and outdoor pools can be closed), a movie theater, a bowling alley, a nature room made of cedar for watching bids and other wildlife, an entertainment room where all the walls are plasma televisions, an exercise center that could rival most health clubs, a gallery where the fine art is displayed and a state-of-the-art security system.

The state-of-the-art security system includes all the basics as well an infrared perimeter control system, the extensive use of closed circuit television cameras, the ability to lock down the gallery with steel shutters for the windows and the doorways, pressure sensitive floor tiles in the gallery and so forth.

With all this security, some expensive jewelry and a number of paintings (not housed in the gallery) disappeared. Wishing to avoid the publicity that comes with calling the police, the owners decide to upgrade the security by adding a team of five security guards patrolling the estate.

A few weeks after the security upgrade, four paintings were stolen from the gallery. Once again, how and who eluded everyone. Any person with any access to the house was screened (including taking a lie detector test) and everyone came up clean. The owners then had a security consultant come in and conduct a security audit. The security consultant was unable to recommend any improvements in the security procedures inside or outside the house. However, on his suggestion, a more extensive and intricate background check was conducted on the employees that also involved an ongoing assessment of the behavior patterns of each employee. This course of action did produce results.

As it turned out, the gardener was the inside man. He had worked for the family for more than a decade and lived on the estate. He was loyal to the family for all this time and would have remained loyal if not for fear for his family back in Mexico. If he did not cooperate, there would be severe consequences for them. Following instructions to the letter, he was able to reconnoiter the estate and the security system. Then he was provided the tools and instruments to disarm the system letting burglars sneak onto the estate and make off with the property.

All these case studies centered on one type of security problem – employing the "wrong" person; a pervasive security problem for the wealthy. What we see in these examples is that one type of security problem can manifest itself in various ways requiring a certain amount of ingenuity and insight to deal with such problems when they arise but, more importantly, to put security solutions in place to avoid them. As it turns out, ingenuity and insight is the sine qua non of effectual security consultants working with high-net-worth clients.

When it comes to the wealthy, their professional and personal circumstances lead to the need for highly customized security solutions thereby negating the ability of anyone, and certainly, any book to provide "the answers." If you, therefore, are looking for tradecraft, you're looking in the wrong place.

This is not a how to book. We do not explain how to modify your schedules to dissuade stalkers. We do not explain how to ameliorate the possibility of someone absconding with and then exploiting your identify. We do not detail how to restructure your real estate holdings to ensure that if a disgruntled ex-spouse seeks to "bleed you dry," it will be impossible to do so. We do not explain how to evaluate the potential and likelihood that someone can and will ghost through your house nor do we detail the appropriate safeguards to make such criminal behavior nearly impossible. As we just noted, this is not a how to book.

A how to book, otherwise known as a self-help book, is anathema to ensure you and what is important to you is safe and sound in today's increasingly dangerous environment. We're big proponents in education and we wrote this book as a first step in that education. There are, however, two "deal breaking" complications when it comes to education.

One is that the ensuring the security of a wealthy family is very often unique that education needs to be highly customized – this book is only an introductory primer. Two, is that the security needs of the wealthy and the very nature of effectively crafting and actualizing appropriate security solutions for high-net-worth individuals will often (but not always) take such solutions way out of the do-it-yourself realm. Just consider the field of technical countermeasure sweeps with the likes of radio frequency spectral analysis and infrared spectral analysis. This type of work tends to be out of the areas of expertise for most of the wealthy.

There are actually quite a number of how to books on the market. And, a few of them have some very good ideas and recommendations in them. But overall, when it comes to people of meaningful wealth, we have found that such information and the erroneous confidence they sometimes instill will often produce more problems then solutions. It's akin to using the internet to diagnose yourself and even prescribe medical treatment. If you were really ill, would it not be wiser to turn to an experienced and knowledgeable physician with all the cutting edge diagnostic tests available as opposed to searching the internet for your malady – and treatment.

On the other hand, if you're seeking an education on the best way to go about understanding a proven methodology for what it takes to craft security solutions for the wealthy, then this book is your introduction. We believe an understanding of this methodology is at the core of the education for the financial elite so that they can make intelligent and informed decisions when it comes to protecting themselves, the ones they love and everything else of real importance to them.

We begin your education with a tour of the problem. We start this tour by tackling the question: "Are you safe?" You might very well be surprised by the answer. In the following chapter, we examine the four protection concerns of the wealthy and center our discussion on the relevant data from our national study of the wealthy.

To maximize your security and the security of the things and people you care about, a well formulated field-proven process is essential. The solution starts with the Personal Protection Process for the wealthy who choose to be proactive when it comes to their security and the security of the people and things important to them. Then in the following chapter on the Crisis Intervention Process is where we address the steps that must to be taken when the unthinkable, the unpalatable and the sometimes unavoidable happens. We close the book with a discussion of the most favorable way to find and select a high-quality security consultant.

Throughout the book we describe situations involving high-net-worth clients. These case studies, which were drawn from our case files and the case files of the niche experts we employ, are intended to be illustrative. In each case we focus on one or a number of specific points. Unfortunately, the real world tends to be much messier. With education as the goal, we find the case studies are a valuable tool to highlight key concepts.

We know that to achieve optimal results it's nearly always best for us to work with intelligent and informed clients. Central to the way we work with our high-net-worth clients is by educating them on the proven methodology described herein. We will also educate them on appropriate security solutions, not so that they can do the job themselves, but so they can make the best possible security related decisions.

That is how to use this book. It's a first step – short and succinct – in gaining an education that will help ensure you and everything you hold dear is Safe & Sound.

Chapter 1

Are You Safe?

Take a moment to consider:

How dangerous is the world today?

Does your wealth make you and your loved ones potential targets?

Let us put it another way:

All in all, how safe are you?

One more question to consider:

Will things get better or worse?

While the odds are that any one individual is safe, the pecuniary success of the wealthy tends to attract the criminal element. By taking rational action, you can further mitigate your low probability of victimization. Moreover, by doing so, you can always pass the "mirror test."

The wealthy tend to perceive themselves as being likely candidates to be targeted by criminals. This perception is in fact magnified with greater wealth.

While there is not a question about the pleasures and privileges of wealth, there is a decided downside to affluence, especially extreme affluence–it can paint a bull's-eye on the back of those who possess it. As we'll see, the wealthy are very sensitive to criminals seeking to separate them from their wealth; and they are justifiably concerned. Before, looking at these perceptions, let us define what we mean by the wealthy–their numbers and aggregate affluence. Let us also consider a few differentiating characteristics separating the financial elite and the rest of the world.

Sizing the World of the Wealthy

The wealthy constitute a unique segment of the population. They are confronted with unique problems as a function of their fortunes as well as unique opportunities, a product of their affluence. When talking about the world of the wealthy, we find that one of the most pervasive questions is: "How many rich people are there?" To answer this question, we developed an analytical model to calculate the size of this corner of the universe.

Sizing the world of significant wealth can be daunting. There is no master list and a great many of the very well-to-do understandably prefer anonymity. As a result, we turned to analytic modeling. The model incorporated data from 133 different sources such as think tanks, financial institutions, industry consultants, academicians, and governmental organizations. The sources included Merrill Lynch, the Spectrem Group, New York University, the Lazard Trust, the Soloton Society, the World Bank, Cornell University, and the International Association for Research in Income and Wealth. (For a detailed explanation of our model and methodology, please refer to **Appendix A: Analytic Modeling Methodology)**

The analytic model allowed us to create a number of possible estimates. In each case, there is a best estimate, a low-end estimate, and a high-end estimate. The accuracy of these various estimates is determined by sensitivity analysis. Prior to examining the estimates in detail, let us delineate the levels within the high-net-worth class (Exhibit 1.1).

Exhibit 1.1: Varieties of Affluence

Level	Wealth Range
Low-End Affluent	$1M to $5M
Affluent	$5M to $25M
Supra-Affluent	$25M to $150M
Mega-Affluent	$150M to $500M
Maxi-Affluent	$500M+

Source: Advanced Planning with the Ultra-Affluent

The low-end affluent have a net-worth of $1 million to $5 million and, for the most part, the members of these families do not consider themselves wealthy—they are often representative of the group known as "middle class millionaires." The affluent control from $5 million to $25 million in assets. According to most financial and legal advisors, we're now starting to talk about the rich. The next three levels–the supra-affluent, the mega-affluent and the maxi-affluent–who have a minimum net-worth of $25 million, comprise the ultra-affluent.

As part of the sizing exercise we were able to calculate how many families were in each of these levels of affluence and our best estimate is that there are more than 17 million families worldwide who are millionaires (Exhibit 1.2). As might be expected, the vast majority are among the low-end affluent and the affluent comprise about half a million families while our best estimate of the ultra-affluent population is 68,570. The wealthy control $69.5 trillion with the ultra-affluent controlling nearly $12 trillion in assets (Exhibit 1.3).

Exhibit 1.2: The Number of Affluent

Level	Low-End Estimate	Best Estimate	High-End Estimate
Low-End Affluent	15,488,000	16,712,000	19,824,000
Affluent	442,680	531,610	645,510
Supra-Affluent	49,220	58,990	62,380
Mega-Affluent	5,670	7,640	8,691
Maxi-Affluent	1,170	1,940	2,580
Total	15,986,740	17,312,180	20,543,161
Ultra-Affluent*	56,060	68,570	73,651

* Includes the Supra-Affluent, the Mega-Affluent, and the Maxi-Affluent

Source: Advanced Planning with the Ultra-Affluent

Exhibit 1.3: The Wealth of the Affluent**

Level	Low-End Estimate	Best Estimate	High-End Estimate
All Affluent	$49.4 Trillion	$69.5 Trillion	$90.9 Trillion
Ultra-Affluent*	$8.4 Trillion	$11.9 Trillion	$13.8 Trillion

* Includes the Supra-Affluent, the Mega-Affluent, and the Maxi-Affluent

** It is important to note that in all of our estimates of assets controlled by the affluent we capped the wealth of the maxi-affluent at $1.2 billion for methodological reasons, though there are clearly many among the ranks of the maxi-affluent who exceeded the cap.

Source: Advanced Planning with the Ultra-Affluent

(Note: Throughout this book, when we refer to the low-end affluent we're talking about people with between $1 million and $5 million. When we use the term affluent, we're talking about people with a net worth of between $5 million and $25 million. When we use the term ultra-affluent we're referring to people with net worth of $25 million or more. When we're talking about people with net worth of $1 million or more we'll refer to them as the wealthy, as high-net-worth or some similar descriptor.)

Distinguishing Characteristics of the Wealthy

The low-end affluent, the affluent and in particular the ultra-affluent are distinguished, first and foremost, by their vast wealth, the simple fact that they have lots of money and can spend it as they wish. Clearly, from the vantage point of criminals seeking to garner some of that wealth as well as others who just identify the wealthy as the enemy, there are quite a number of potential victims commanding sizable assets.

Aside from significant monies per se, there are other characteristics of the wealthy especially the wealthy with greater financial resources. The wealthy are also characterized by how they have adapted to the particular situation of being rich. This does not mean that other demographic, economic, social, or cultural populations do not share the characteristics; only that these adaptations are more pronounced and typical among the wealthy. These characteristics are:

Considerable personal/financial complexity.

A desire to influence their world.

A robust preference to work with the best.

Complexity. Simply stated, the fact that the wealthy have more money religiously makes their personal and financial lives more complicated. They have more things to take care of—more assets, more houses, more financial demands from loved ones and so forth. External macro-environmental factors such as tax laws, a litigious society, disgruntled employees, terrorist hot spots and the like also tend to play a far larger role in their lives than they do in the less wealthy. The very parameters that constrain them and the options that are available to them create significant complexity.

Another area of intense complexity is created by family and personal dealings. The family dynamic is ever-complicated, and money often magnifies eccentricities and animosities. Older children (the operative word here being children), for instance, expressing the position that they can care for themselves while placing themselves in clearly potentially dangerous situations makes protecting them an ever more arduous undertaking.

Influence. Money and power walk hand in hand, so it's no surprise that the financial elite are often focused on ensuring appropriate levels of control over their immediate environments. They frequently want to exercise a measure of influence over just about every situation of considerable significance in their lives.

Needless to say, when the complexity of their lives already referred to meets the need for influence head-on, life can become very convoluted for the wealthy. When, for example, the objective is total safety for loved ones—as it often is expressed— here are usually an array of conflicts in trying to come as close as possible to such an impossibility. In the context of ensuring the safety of the family, influence is demonstrated by the way their fortunes are used to meet the various security needs, in particular when there are issues of dominance being played out within a family.

Only the best. With money comes many privileges, and working with exceptional security consultants is–or cancertainly be–one of those privileges. When it comes to obtaining expertise concerning this aspect of their lives, the wealthy are unquestionably searching for the best as there is a great deal at stake. The wealthy generally recognize the need to pay for this level of expertise, and as they are paying well, they expect–and rightfully so–a very high degree of professionalism and competence.

The corollary of paying for the top-notch security consultants is their insistence on getting a top-notch security consultant. In effect, the wealthy are more demanding and particular–a trend that is only intensifying. While the wealthy choose to work with the best-of-the-best, as we'll see in

Chapter 5: Caveat Emptor that this is not always the case. In fact, present day, not working with top-of-the-line security consultants is unfortunately likely to be the norm.

We bring these characteristics to your attention, for although they might not be characteristic of you, they are generally characteristic of the wealthy. Moreover, they prove to be instrumental for us–to varying degrees–when we work with the wealthy on crafting and implementing security solutions.

With our brief overview of the wealthy–their numbers, their aggregate wealth and some of their key defining characteristics–completed, we're now on the same page when we're talking about the financial elite. We now turn to their overall perception of their safety as a function of their affluence.

Considerable Monies Breed Concern

For the most part, the wealthy are sensitive to the fact that their financial position can readily make them a target for the more nefarious among us. To move beyond anecdotes and derive a detailed empirical understanding of the wealthy, we conducted an extensive survey of 427 wealthy individuals (For a detailed explanation of the research methodology and demographics, please refer to **Appendices B: Sampling Methodology** and **Appendix C: High-net-worth Sample Demographics**). (We report the findings of this program of research extensively in the following chapter and throughout the book as appropriate.)

For the wealthy, the world is a dangerous place. Three out of four of the wealthy (74.5%) have this view of the world (Exhibit 1.4). More telling is that 54.6 percent of them say that their affluence makes them a special target. A similar percentage (53.5%) attribute their position in society to making them a potential target.

Exhibit 1.4: The Impact of Wealth

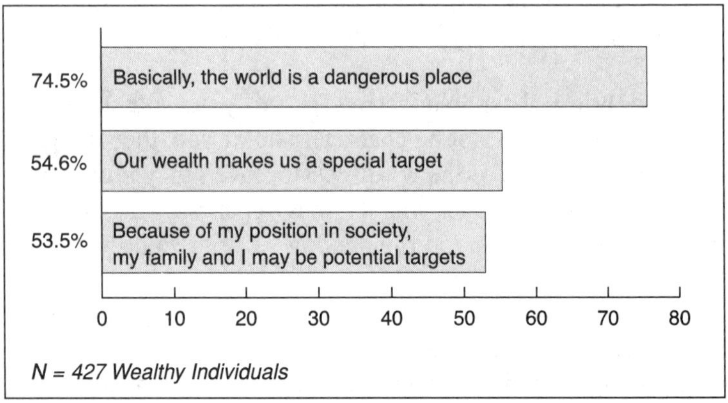

Statistically, the same percentages of the various wealth segments see the world as a dangerous place (Exhibit 1.5). However, when we look at the other two issues, we can readily see that the more affluent a person is, the more inclined they are to see the direct downside of their wealth. In other words, more money translates into more worry when it comes to security and with good reason. While the low-end affluent are indeed concerned, the proportion of the affluent and ultra-affluent are much more so.

While less than a quarter of the low-end affluent (22.8%) see their position in society making them a potential target, more than half the affluent (59.2%) and nearly four out of five of the ultra-affluent (78.5%) see their position in society making them a potential target. More money translates into a criminal thinking: "more for the taking." Also, with greater pecuniary achievements, the wealthy garner a higher profile which they conclude draws unwanted attention.

Addressing the point more explicitly, 28.2 percent of the low-end affluent identify their wealth as making them a special target. This percentage balloons to 71.8 percent for the affluent and nearly all the ultra-affluent (92.4%) feel this way. The possession of extreme wealth translates into the perception of being a shining golden target to criminals.

Exhibit 1.5: The Impact of Wealth by Level of Wealth

Issue	Low-end Affluent	Affluent	Ultra-affluent
Basically, the world is a dangerous place	73.3%	76.1%	74.7%
Because of my position in society, my family and I may be potential targets	22.8%	59.2%	78.5%
Our wealth makes us a special target	28.2%	71.8%	92.4%

N = 427 Wealthy Individuals

What is even more troubling is that the financial elite do not anticipate a correction in the level or persistence of security treats they confront (Exhibit 1.6). Irrespective of level of affluence, there is a general consensus (89.2%) that the situation will only worsen. Threats from terrorism to child kidnapping and from identify theft to burglaries, are being recognized as part of the very fabric of their social environment.

Exhibit 1.6: The Wealthy Believe the Situation Will Only Worsen

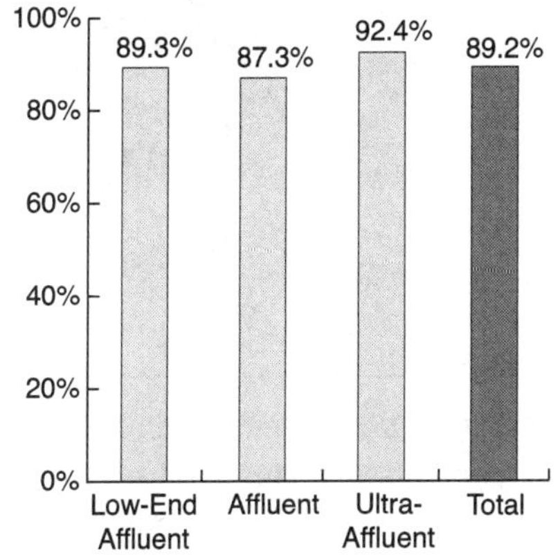

N = 427 Wealthy Individuals

The Impact of "Sudden Wealth"

What we can conclude from the research is that the wealthy see the world as a dangerous place and that their affluence makes them a target. This perspective was reinforced in another study of 87 inheritors where we observed that newly acquired wealth results in a greater sensitivity to security needs.

Each participant in this research program inherited between $7.5 million and $9.4 million in the previous two years. Before they inherited, none of them had more than $100,000 in savings or investments, none of them owned their houses outright and none of them were earning incomes in excess of $60,000 per year. Moreover, none of them reported being particularly concerned about their personal safety or the safety of their loved ones. In effect, before becoming millionaires, these individuals did not see themselves as targets. However, after inheriting, 67.8 percent reported being "very" or "extremely" concerned about their personal safety of the safety of their loved ones (Exhibit 1.7)

Exhibit 1.7: Sudden Wealth Generates Security Concerns

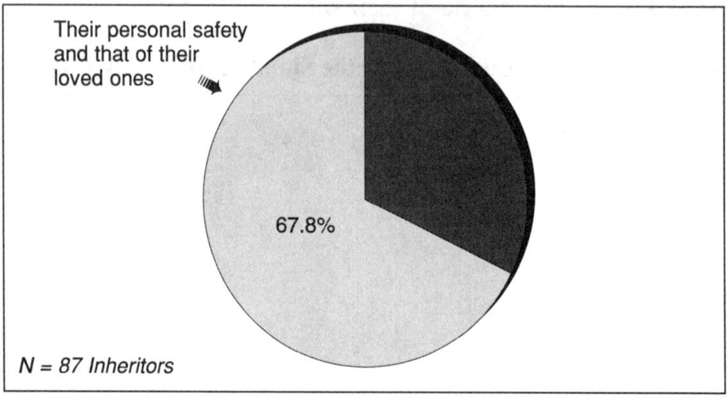

As noted, a downside to being wealthy is that criminals want to share in your good fortune – to your detriment. The majority of people who suddenly become wealthy, as in the case of an inheritance, quickly confront this reality.

Being Famous Generates Concern

We have seen that the wealthy–including newly minted millionaires–are justifiably concerned about their security. And, we have seen that with greater affluence, there is greater concern. Along the same lines, celebrity proves to be a stronger and stronger magnet for attracting the attention of criminals.

We empirically came to this conclusion based on a survey of 31 entertainment and sports agents and business mangers. To be included in the study, each of these professionals were required to have a minimum of 20 celebrity clients who had a net-worth of $20 million or more. We asked them to identify the number of incidents of selected security problems faced by their wealthy celebrity clients in 2000 and presently.

We found there was a tremendous increase in security problems confronting wealthy celebrities today than just four years ago. Incidents of stalking requiring legal and protective actions were up 210 percent. Incidences of a celebrity's identity being stolen were up 80 percent. Frivolous lawsuits filed against celebrities were up proportionately the most at 370 percent. Meanwhile, attacks on property (i.e., burglaries, vandalism) were up 190 percent.

Exhibit 1.8: Identified Significant Increases among Their Financially Successful Clients

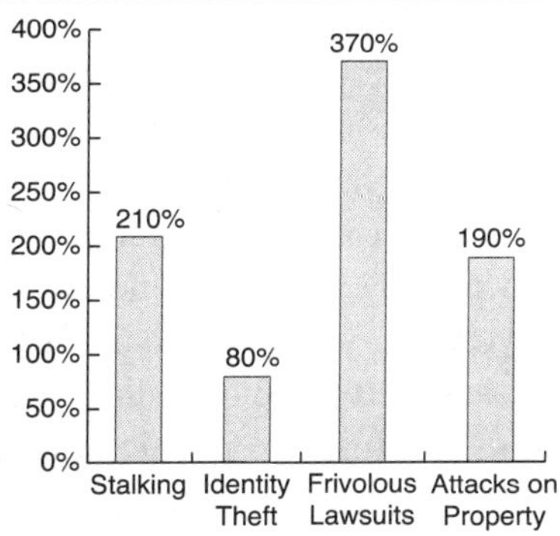

N = 31 entertainment and sports agents and business mangers

Without doubt, more than ever before, being famous draws the attention and interest of the unscrupulous element of society. Being rich and famous just magnifies the problem. The entertainment and sports agents and business managers noted that their well-to-do celebrity clients are more concerned and anxious than ever about security issues.

What we can deduce from these three research studies is the high correlation between affluence and the recognition that the world is threatening. It's not that those of less financial stature cannot be victims as well. Certainly they can and are. It's just that greater wealth regularly makes for a better more attractive target. This is the macro-perspective. When it comes to any particular wealthy individual, when it comes to you, the bottom line issue is: "Are you safe?"

Are You Safe?

The numbers are shared with all of us fairly regularly. For instance, approximately 40,000 people die each year in the United States in automobile crashes, and a multiple of that number are seriously injured. Along the same lines, any American today is a million times more likely to die in a car accident than a terrorist attack. This goes for the wealthy as well. But, for the wealthy, these statistics often belie the point.

One of our ultra-affluent clients is a professional gambler. In the late 1990s, he preferred blackjack where he was the member of a very successful card counting team. Blackjack was the source of his first few million dollars. Now a days, with the sophistication of the casinos, his game of choice is poker. He equates life to playing cards: "Some days you lose, other days you win. If you can, you do everything you can – everything legal that is – to better the odds that you win." Whether it's counting cards or reading people, his experience and expertise gives him a professional edge that has translated into many millions of dollars in his pocket.

The same holds true when dealing with the security needs of the wealthy. As a person with significant affluence, you can often exponentially better your odds of avoiding security problems such as the abduction of your child or grandchild, or the loss of a valuable painting as well as responding to problems with tremendous expertise and "firepower" when crises unfortunately occur. What does this mean? **It means you can use a sliver of your wealth to make certain you and all you hold dear are well protected and that you can respond appropriately in times of crisis.**

While your financial success provides you the ability to create a stronger and more extensive zone of protection around you and those people and things you hold dear, the question really is "Should you spend the time, effort and money to do so?" So, back to the question: "Are you safe?"

The simple answer is: "Yes." Yes, you're safe. If you consider the matter statistically, there is a higher probability that you will die in your sleep at a ripe old age than be killed by burglars who you stumbled upon while they were taking your prized Monet off your living room wall.

The slightly longer answer is: "Maybe." Maybe you're safe. While it's very unlikely that you'll lose your wealth in a hedge fund that turns out to be nothing more than a Ponzi scheme or that you're hijacked while flying on your private jet the possibility exists and possibilities like these are increasing in likelihood pretty much daily.

The real question should be: "Are you as safe as you can reasonably be?" Regrettably, for most of the wealthy the answer is "No." That is, you can probably increase the probability that nothing will happen to you or those you care about. In our experience, there are few situations where the wealthy could not take steps to mitigate the possibility something adverse happening (see **Chapter 3: The Protection Planning Process**).

Passing the "Mirror Test"

Should we extend time to infinity, then by ergodicity, every bad thing that can happen will happen. While we have found it's often possible to meaningfully, and sometimes dramatically, enhance the security of the wealthy, complete bullet proof security is an impossibility.

If someone wants to really hurt you or your loved ones; if someone wants to know your deepest and darkest secrets badly enough; if someone truly wants to abscond with your wealth; if someone wants to take your valuable property; that someone with the right incentives, with the right tools and processes, with the right expertise and talent, will. At the same time, what you can do is take action such that you're meaningfully increasing the odds of anything happening; increasing the odds – which are high to begin with – that you and those you care about as well as your possessions are as safe as reasonably possible.

One of our high-net-worth clients explained it to us as the "mirror test." If something BAD happened; if a family member was violently attacked by a stalker, if lewd pictures of your underage grandchildren appeared on the internet, if you lost a merit less lawsuit brought by an angry and delusional ex-spouse, if your 30 foot yacht was looted while in dry dock, can you look in the mirror and say, "I did everything reasonably possible?"

It's not rational to think anyone can cover all the bases; to ensure absolute security no matter what. And, that is not the purpose of implementing security solutions. Broadly speaking, your goal is to make the odds of something BAD happening as low as possible while being realistic.

In **Chapter 3: The Protection Planning Process**, we describe two of the conceptual algorithms we employ to be "realistic." These conceptual algorithms also prove useful ensuring you do not fall into the abyss of irrational paranoia and conclude that the only way to be safe and sound is to sequester yourself in a nicely equipped, exceptionally well furnished underground bunker in a nearly impossible to find location surrounded by the latest in both lethal and non-lethal antipersonnel devices. Consequently, if you have taken all reasonable actions to decrease the odds of something BAD happening and something BAD does happen, you can look at yourself in the mirror and say: "I did what I could?" Furthermore, if something BAD does indeed occur, you're prepared by having a crisis intervention plan in place which is set to go instantly when you activate it (see **Chapter 4: The Crisis Intervention Process).** Now you passed the "mirror test."

Before we explain these processes, it's worthwhile for you to see how you compare to your peers when it comes to your concerns about security. This is the focus of the next chapter.

Chapter 2

Protection Concerns of the Wealthy

Think for a moment:

Who is really important to you?

> How would you feel if something horrible happened to him or her?

What secret do you have which you strongly prefer to remain secret?

> How would you feel if that secret was disclosed in an email blast to everyone you knew?

Have you ever been involved in an unjust lawsuit?

> How would you feel if you were involved in an unjust lawsuit and a sizable portion of your wealth was stolen from you in the settlement?

What property do you own such as a painting, jewelry, a house that is really important to you?

> How would you feel if something horrible happened to it?

As a group, the wealthy tend to be concerned, first and foremost, about the security of their loved ones, then themselves. They're also concerned about their private information staying that way and ensuring "thieves" don't "take" them and their property.

Protection concerns are those "buckets" or sets of concerns easily characterized that are, or may be important, and are at risk. We have identified four such buckets that are critical to the wealthy. They are:

- **The security of your person and your loved one.** For most of us, when it comes to our own well personal being, or more poignantly the well being of those we hold dear, there is nothing more important. Making sure the people we care greatly about as well as ourselves is religiously the most important protection concern among the high-net-worth.

- **Keeping confidential information confidential.** There are very few psychological exhibitionists in the world. If you're like the majority of the ultra-affluent, the affluent or even those less fiscally endowed, you do not want strangers knowing what videos you rent, how much money you have and where it is, or your medical history.

- **Making sure your wealth is not stolen from you.** It has taken time and, usually considerable effort and commitment to amass substantial monies. And, even if your wealth was handed to you by birthright, you probably want to keep it. In fact, in all the research we have conducted on the topic we have never found anyone who was okay with the idea of their wealth being stolen from them by vindictive ex-spouses, con artists or some other variety of criminal.

- **Making sure property is safe.** You probably own real estate such as the house you live in. You might own a yacht, a piece of a plane or even a whole plane. Your family is likely to have some expensive jewelry and heirlooms that might not be costly but have tremendous personal value. The objective is to make sure all these things are neither vandalized nor absconded with.

These four sets of protection concerns interrelate. For example, making sure your house is protected from burglars, or making sure people do not know your secrets all help to make sure you and your loved ones are safe and sound. While it proves useful to be able to examine each of these protection concerns on their own when you implement various security solutions, you're often going to also be making some other aspect of your life more secure.

Turning to the research, we find that the order we just described the protection concerns is the order the wealthy identify as being the most potentially anxiety producing as well as most important to attend to (Exhibit 2.1). Based on our national study of the wealthy, employing a distributive forced choice methodology, the highest ranked protection concern was protecting themselves and their loved ones (the weighted composite score was an 8.91 out of a possible weighted composite score of 10). Next on the list is protecting their confidential information with a weighted composite score of 8.06 followed by protecting their wealth (weighted composite score = 7.92). Finally, there was protecting their property with a weighted composite score of 7.13.

With the distributive forced choice methodology we used to derive the ranking of protection concerns any weighted composite score above a 6.50 is very significant. That means that each and every protection concern is an imperative issue to the research participants–the rich people. No one wants something to happen to themselves or their loved ones. They want to maintain control over confidential information. They want to keep their wealth out of the hands of thieves. And, they do not want anything to happen to their property.

All in all, the financial elite want to be protected against criminals in a big way. This does not in any way imply that those not so financially endowed are also not seeking such protection. It's just that the wealthy are.

Exhibit 2.1: Ranking the Protection Concerns

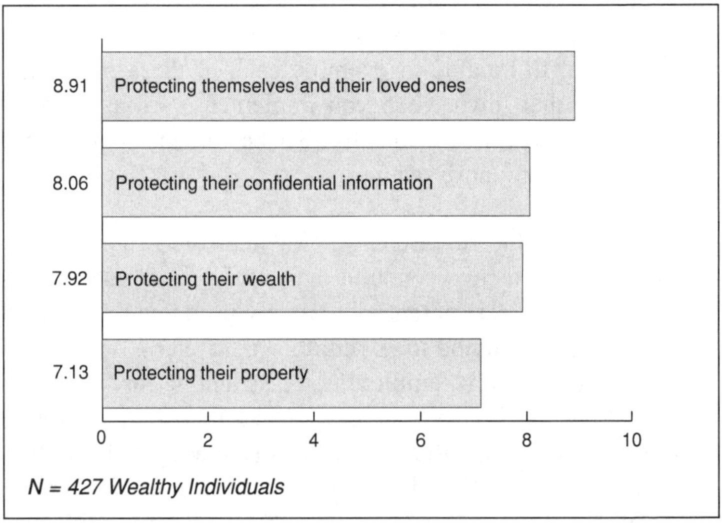

This ranking is a function of asking the wealthy to make comparisons among the various sets of protection concerns. In the national study, we also chose to drill down by requesting the wealthy survey participants to decide if the are "very" or "extremely" concerned about a particular security issue or not. Let us now examine their responses.

As we go through their answers, take a moment and think about how you would have responded. In other words, are you "very" or "extremely" concerned about each specific protection need we will recount? In this way you're benchmarking yourself against your peers.

Personal Protection and Protection for Their Loved Ones

At the top of the list of fears for the wealthy is something happening to them or, more importantly, those people they care deeply about. While the probability may be quite small, the consequences are usually gargantuan.

As we see in Exhibit 2.2, when it comes to themselves–the wealthy respondents personally–the greatest concern is traveling internationally (49.4%). This concern was more pronounced among a larger percentage of the ultra-affluent (68.4%) compared to the affluent (52.1%) compared to the low-end affluent (40.3%). With the very visible and sometimes violent problems throughout the world coupled with the fact that the wealthy are nevertheless globetrotting makes many of them understandably anxious.

Predators are a meaningful concern for a fifth of the wealthy surveyed (21.2%). There are significant differences among the levels of affluence on this topic. Nearly half the ultra-affluent (48.1%) are worried about predators. This is, in part, a function of their generally higher profile. Meanwhile, 21.8 percent of the affluent and only 10.2 percent of the low-end affluent are "extremely" or "very" concerned about predators targeting them.

In total, 13.8 percent of the wealthy are meaningfully concerned about acts of violence committed against them. Somewhat fewer wealthy individuals are "very" or "extremely" concerned about traveling domestically (12.6%), robberies or muggings (8.4%) and being kidnapped (4.7%). The pattern where greater wealth results in a higher proportion of each segment of affluence is evidenced with each of these concerns.

Exhibit 2.2 Personal Protection Concerns

Concerns	Low-end affluent	Affluent	Ultra-affluent	Total
Security when traveling internationally	40.3%	52.1%	68.4%	49.4%
Predators	10.2%	21.8%	48.1%	21.1%
Acts of violence against you	11.2%	13.4%	21.5%	13.8%
Security when traveling domestically	7.8%	15.5%	20.3%	12.6%
Robbery or mugging	5.3%	9.9%	13.9%	8.4%
Personally being abducted	1.0%	5.6%	12.7%	4.7%

N = 427 Wealthy Individuals

Save for traveling internationally, about a fifth or less of the wealthy surveyed are concerned about their personal security. However, the picture changes dramatically, when we're talking about their loved ones (Exhibit 2.3).

Irrespective of level of wealth, about four out of five of the wealthy are significantly concerned about predators targeting their loved ones (77.5%). With feelings and obligations of responsibility for the safety of their loved ones, these wealthy individuals are very anxious because they realize the tremendous harm a predator can do. Also, with the increase in preditorial behavior such as the boon in sexual predators targeting children through the Internet, the greater majority of the wealthy rightfully are concerned about their loved ones.

Highly correlated with anxiety over predators is anxiety about a loved one being abducted (57.1%). Greater affluence results in this concern being more prominent. Nearly seven out of ten (68.4%) of the ultra-affluent are "extremely" or "very" concerned about a loved one being abducted. This is clearly a function of their financial position. A slightly smaller percentage (59.2%) of the affluent and relatively fewer still of the low-end affluent (51.5%) are anxious when it comes to one of their loved ones being taken. While the odds are low, we know all too well that the kidnapping of a child or grandchild can immediately send a well-to-do parent or grandparent into near catatonic shock. The advent and explosive growth of child abduction insurance policies is indicative of this growing and pressing concern.

Along the same lines, 56.7 percent of the wealthy are significantly concerned that their loved ones would be victims of violence and 35.4 percent are similarly concerned that their loved ones would be victims of a robbery or mugging. Because of the greater frequency of these events in general, proportionately more of the wealthy are "accepting" of them.

Only 15.7 percent and 11.5 percent of the wealthy are meaningfully concerned about their loved ones traveling–in order–internationally or domestically. If there is a potential issue with travel, it's easy to reschedule. Therefore, fewer of the wealthy–because of the amount of control they can exert in this area–are "very" or "extremely" concerned.

Exhibit 2.3 Protection Concerns for Loved Ones

Concerns	Low-end affluent	Affluent	Ultra-affluent	Total
Predators	78.2%	76.8%	77.2%	77.5%
A loved one being abducted	51.5%	59.2%	68.4%	57.1%
Acts of violence against a loved one	52.9%	59.2%	62.0%	56.7%
Robbery or mugging	31.1%	38.0%	41.8%	35.4%
Security when they travel internationally	5.3%	22.5%	30.4%	15.7%
Security when they travel domestically	11.2%	12.0%	11.4%	11.5%

N = 427 Wealthy Individuals

We first saw it in the **How to Use This Book** section. A goodly number of the security crises the wealthy face are predicated on the "wrong" people having access to them and their property. It can be the nanny or the celebrity assistant or the gardener. Letting the "wrong" people "in" can easily lead to disaster. While adroit pre-screening as well as ongoing screenings can viably mitigate the possibility of a crisis, only 37.9 percent of the wealthy are "extremely" or "very" concerned about hiring unscrupulous people who will have access to their homes and family (Exhibit 2.4). About half the ultra-affluent (53.2%) and affluent (46.5%) feel this way. Meanwhile, only about one quarter (26.2%) of the low-end affluent see this as a major concern.

Exhibit 2.4: Concerned about Hiring Unscrupulous People Who Will Have Access to Their Homes and/or Family

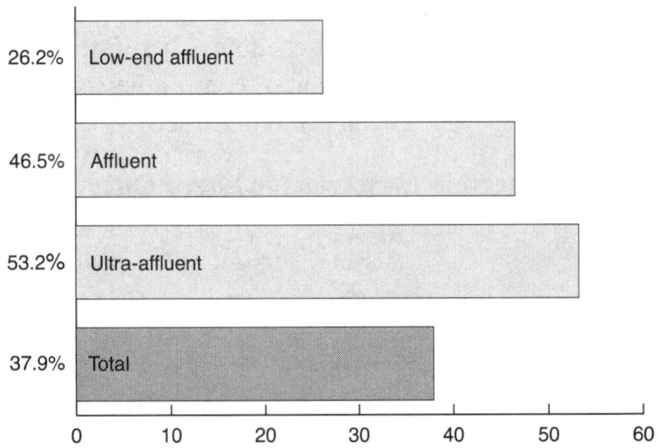

N = 427 Wealthy Individuals

What we see in the research is that many of the wealthy–those people who have principal control over their family fortunes–are not particularly worried about their own safety. On the other hand, a significantly greater number of them are very concerned about the safety of their loved ones. Consider the potential of being abducted. Only 4.7 percent of the wealthy found this issue a meaningful concern when it was about them, but 57.1 percent saw it as a significant concern when it had to do with a loved one.

Only travel–in particular, international travel–was a bigger concern to the wealthy survey respondents personally than it's to them as it relates to their loved ones. A contributing reason for this is that many of the wealthy survey respondents need to travel for business where their loved ones rarely do. The interplay of the twin dynamic of control (see **Chapter 1: Are you Safe?**) and the assumed role of "guardian" is the primary reason for the wealthy being more concerned about the safety of their loved ones then about their own safety.

Protecting Their Confidential Information

In many ways, we're living in a world without secrets. From hackers "strolling" into secure data bases to people handing over information that leads to someone stealing their identity, it's more common than ever before for confidential information to no longer be private.

After the security of their loved ones and their own well being, the wealthy are concerned about protecting their confidential information (Exhibit 2.5). The major concern is identity theft (77.5%). The greater majority of the ultra-affluent (83.5%) and about three-quarters of both the affluent (74.6%) and low-end affluent (77.2%) are "extremely" or "very" concerned about their identities being stolen and a criminal exploiting the situation for financial gain.

Identity theft is one of the fastest growing crimes in our society. It's very likely that the wealthy survey participants have either directly been victims of identity theft of are personally aware of someone who was. The pervasiveness and the potential "damage" identity theft can cause instill in the wealthy a healthy sense of dread.

Moving on, about two-fifths of the wealthy (42.6%) are "very" or "extremely" concerned about someone gaining access to their private business information. As business interests prove to be critical to entering and remaining in the ranks of the financial elite (see **Appendix C: High-net-worth Sample Demographics)** the fact that those of greater affluence are more concerned is only logical.

Someone gaining access to their medical records is a significant concern to 41.0 percent of the wealthy. What is telling is that the different levels of affluence are percentage wise, all about the same with regard to this concern. Apparently irrespective of level of affluence, those people with medical histories do not want strangers knowing about them.

Overall, 40.7 percent of the wealthy are meaningfully concerned about someone seeking to damage their personal and professional reputation. What is quite interesting about this particular concern is that proportionately the affluent are most sensitive to the matter (50.7%). In contrast both the low-end affluent (35.4%) and the ultra-affluent (36.7%) are relatively less concerned. For the low-end affluent as well as the ultra-affluent the rationale is that relatively fewer of them can be badly "hurt" in this manner.

A little more than a quarter of the wealthy (26.9%) are meaningfully concerned about someone eaves dropping on them or their loved ones. Here, we return to the dominant pattern of greater affluence being proportionately more concerned (36.7% of the ultra-affluent; 26.1% of the affluent; 23.8% of the low-end affluent). The relatively low percentages we understand to be a function of the perceived very low probability of occurrence.

Lastly, only 8.0 percent of the wealthy are "very" or "extremely" concerned about extortion. There is proportionately much greater concern among the ultra-affluent (16.5%) than among the affluent (8.5%) or the low-end affluent (4.4%). This is more of a function of being able to be pressured due to indiscretions than of harboring horrendous secrets.

Exhibit 2.5 Protection Concerns Dealing with Confidential Information

Concerns	Low-end affluent	Affluent	Ultra-affluent	Total
Identity theft	77.2%	74.6%	83.5%	77.5%
Someone gaining access to their private business information	25.2%	55.6%	64.6%	42.6%
Someone gaining access to their or their loved ones medical records	40.8%	41.5%	40.5%	41.0%
Someone seeking to damage their personal or professional reputation	35.4%	50.7%	36.7%	40.7%
Someone eaves dropping on them or their loved ones	23.8%	26.1%	36.7%	26.9%
Extortion	4.4%	8.5%	16.5%	8.0%

N = 427 Wealthy Individuals

In sum, the most pervasive protection concern of the wealthy with respect to confidential information is identity theft; the damage can be extreme and the likelihood of occurrence is ever growing. Nevertheless, for two-fifths of the financial elite, a person gaining access to private business information or medical information as well as someone seeking information that can be used to damage a personal or professional reputation is a major concern.

Protecting Their Wealth

In most instances, it's so very arduous to amass a real fortune—to join the ranks of the low-end affluent, more so the affluent and, even more so, the ultra-affluent. All the while, fortunes can easily be made to vanish; sometimes through mismanagement and sometimes because of one type of thief or another.

As we see in Exhibit 2.6, the most pervasive concern among the wealthy when it comes to protecting their wealth is the fear that someone would take advantage of their children or grandchildren for financial gain (72.6%). Nine out of ten of the ultra-affluent (91.1%), three-quarters of the affluent (75.4%) and about a third of the low-end affluent (63.6%) feel this way.

Many of the wealthy clearly hold to the idea that some criminal will see their offspring or the offspring of their offspring and think of them as the keys to the family fortune–or at least the monies these junior family members have access to. This perspective ties back to the greater concern the wealthy have for the physical safety of their loved ones than for their own (see above). We find that while the wealthy are well founded in this concern, relatively few of them are taking appropriate steps to mitigate the potential problem.

Many of the financial elite (67.9%) are "very" or "extremely" concerned about being targeted by unfounded or frivolous lawsuits from people they know such as ex-spouses, ex-employees, former business associates and the like. A larger percentage of the ultra-affluent (83.5%) feel this way compared to the affluent (68.3%) and the low-end affluent (61.7%). In the same vein, 58.5 percent of the wealthy are concerned about being sued by people they do not know.

There is no doubt that we live in a very litigious society where the wealthy are regularly seen as being a meal ticket for the immoral and deceitful who readily use the court system as a weapon of mass destruction. Consequently, the well-to-do are indeed often the target of frivolous and unfounded lawsuits that are more terrorist weapon than valid grievance – and the financial elite are all too familiar with this problem.

Nearly half the wealthy are "very" or "extremely" concerned about embezzlement at the firms they own or work at. This is more the case with the ultra-affluent (68.4%), than with the affluent (50.7%), and least with the low-end affluent (39.3%). There is a direct relationship between equity in a business entity and their disquiet about embezzlement.

Overall, a similar percentage of the wealthy are concerned about doing business with unscrupulous people (46.6%). Proportionately more of the ultra-affluent (51.9%) feel this way than the affluent (47.2%) or the low-end affluent (42.2%). Sensitivity to fraud in business is center stage today. From being personally "burnt" in business dealings to knowing someone who has been, more and more of the wealthy have become increasingly anxious and circumspect about whom they do business with.

Only one in ten of the wealthy (10.1%) are "very" or "extremely" concerned about being the victim of a financial fraud. There is not a statistically significant difference among the three levels of affluence. In general, the financial elite expect the array of professional and financial advisors they employ to protect them from this problem.

Finally, a mere 5.4 percent of the wealthy are meaningfully concerned about hiring an unscrupulous financial advisor. Relatively more of the ultra-affluent (13.9%) feel this way compared to 6.3 percent for the affluent and 1.5 percent for the low-end affluent. This is a function of the way they tend to find their financial advisors – through referrals.

Exhibit 2.6 Protection Concerns Dealing with Wealth

Concerns	Low-end affluent	Affluent	Ultra-affluent	Total
Someone taking advantage of their children or grandchildren for financial gain	63.6%	75.4%	91.1%	72.6%
Being targeted by unfounded or frivolous lawsuits by people they know	61.7%	68.3%	83.5%	67.9%
Being targeted by unfounded or frivolous lawsuits by people they do not know	50.5%	57.7%	81.0%	58.5%
Embezzlement at work	39.3%	50.7%	68.4%	48.5%
Doing business with unscrupulous people	42.2%	47.2%	51.9%	46.6%
Being the victim of a financial fraud	10.2%	9.9%	10.1%	10.1%
Hiring unscrupulous financial advisors	1.5%	6.3%	13.9%	5.4%

N = 427 Wealthy Individuals

The biggest worry among the wealthy is for their progeny. From children and grandchildren they see as not having enough experience "in the real world" to a lack of financial sophistication to just being a little naïve, they realize them as a weakness, a potential breach in their financial fortresses.

Another area where they see the criminals on the horizon deals with the deluge of lawsuits that are insidious in our society. While you worked hard to acquire and maintain your wealth, there are people all over who look at using the courts as a way for them to play the litigation lottery.

What is so unfortunate is that this set of protection concerns is the only one of the four where it's indeed possible to dramatically moderate if not ostensibly eliminate the threat and, in our experience, the requisite actions are rarely taken. A small amount of cleverness added to a considerable amount of cutting edge asset protection planning goes a very long way to mitigating unfounded and frivolous lawsuits. At the same time, taking the time and effort to know who children and grandchildren as well as who you're dealing with – business associates, advisors, whomever – will also greatly diminish the possibility of interacting or doing business with the wrong people.

Protecting Their Property

It's quite common for the wealthy to take many of the necessary precautions to protect their property. There is almost always an alarm system in every house and valuables are often kept in safe deposit boxes. Still, many of the wealthy are concerned about protecting their property.

In total, 56.0 percent of the wealthy are "very" or "extremely" concerned about their house(s) being burglarized (Exhibit 2.7). About half the low-end affluent (50.5%) and half the affluent (52.1%) feel this way. In contrast, 77.2 percent of the ultra-affluent are meaningfully concerned about burglaries. Close behind, is their concern over vandalism to their homes (52.5%) with the same relative percentages among the three levels of affluence.

When it comes to their property, the wealthy are–as a group–habitually centered on their houses. For the majority of them their houses are not only large investments, they reflect their personalities as well as serve as a psychological foundation–a touchstone in a scary world. Many of the wealthy feel a deep sense of violation when their houses are invaded or desecrated in any way.

In order then comes concern over the loss of valuables such as jewelry, art work and even pets (29.7%). The ultra-affluent are most concerned (64.6%) which is a product of having the most valuables and generally the most expensive valuables. Meanwhile, 29.6 percent of the affluent and 16.5 percent of the low-end affluent are also "very" or "extremely" concerned.

Vandalism to their property aside from their homes is a meaningful concern to 26.9 percent of the wealthy. Again, a larger percentage of the ultra-affluent are seriously concerned (62.0%) than the other two levels of affluence (31.0% for the affluent; 10.7% for the low-end affluent). These percentages reflect the more financially successful having more property at risk such as a private plane or a Renoir.

One-fifth (20.6%) of the wealthy are meaningfully concerned about transporting valuable property such as jewelry or critical documents. Nearly half the ultra-affluent (49.4%), about a fifth of the affluent (21.8%) and 8.7 percent of the low-end affluent feel this way. The downside of losing these items or them being stolen is so great that transporter services are religiously hired.

Exhibit 2.7 Protection Concerns Dealing with Property

Concerns	Low-end affluent	Affluent	Ultra-affluent	Total
Their house(s) being burglarized	50.5%	52.1%	77.2%	56.0%
Vandalism to their house(s)	48.1%	47.9%	72.2%	52.5%
Loss of valuables such as jewelry, art work, pets and so forth	16.5%	29.6%	64.6%	29.7%
Vandalism to other property such as cars, planes, yachts and art work	10.7%	31.0%	62.0%	26.9%
Transporting valuable property or documents	8.7%	21.8%	49.4%	20.6%

N = 427 Wealthy Individuals

While the least important of the four protection concerns, protecting property still is quite important with the wealthy concerned over their houses topping the list. In many respects, by taking the requisite steps to protect your property you're also protecting the security of yourself and your loved ones.

From Statistics to You

From the perspective of our high-net-worth client security consulting business, it's essential that we have our hand on the pulse of the private wealth market. Nationwide research such as this provides us with a macro-perspective of the protection concerns of the wealthy. It's useful to us in trend analysis and is one of the approaches we employ to stay at the cutting edge.

For you, these research findings can provide a frame reference. As we said in the beginning of the chapter: "How concerned are you with respect to each of the specific security concerns?"

You can now benchmark yourself. You can see how your concerns compare to other people in a similar financial position. Our intent here is to provide you with perspective. However, you need to always keep in mind that statistics such as these only provide a macro-perspective. What is critically important is your unique situation.

We now turn to what you can do. We begin with the proactive action you can take (**Chapter 3: The Protection Planning Process**). From there, we move to what can be done in times of a security emergency (**Chapter 4: The Crisis Intervention Process**). We conclude with what you should be aware of in selecting a security consultant (**Chapter 5: Caveat Emptor**).

Chapter 3

The Protection Planning Process

Have you ever thought about what you need to know in order to ensure the safety of your family?

Have you ever thought about what you're willing to "put up with" in order to be safer?

Have you ever thought about what trade offs you would make between security and cost?

Have you ever thought about when your security precautions go "stale?"

Have you ever thought about how to make all your security solutions operate synergistically?

The Protection Planning Process is at the heart of ensuring the security of yourself, your loves ones, your confidential information, your wealth and your property. The Protection Planning Process moves from the fact-finding phase, to an evaluation of various security solutions, the creation of an action plan to implementation and follow through which incorporates an ongoing review of your changing security needs. While conceptually formal, the process is easily mutable to the needs, concerns and interests of the wealthy.

In order to realistically ensure your security, we need a core process. There must to be an overall systematic methodology that provides a way to examine your situation and applying state-of-the-art security solutions taking into account your complete or selected protection concerns. The Protection Planning Process fits the bill perfectly. The Protection Planning Process is one through which you and your security consultant can best identify and implement an Action Plan that is completely in accord with your protection objectives. Through the Protection Planning Process you, working with your security consultant, craft, implement and remain diligent with respect to your security solutions.

The Process

Operationally, the Protection Planning Process is composed of six phases – (1) the At Risk Assessment, (2) Evaluate Security Solutions, (3) Select Security Solutions, (4) the Action Plan, (5) Implementation and (6) Follow Through. However, while we can identify distinct phases, you're not easily pigeonholed and processed; you have a variety of protection needs and disparate ideas and feelings about various types of threats. The possibility of being the target of various types of criminals also varies. So the Protection Planning Process should not be perceived as a strictly observed, incontrovertible process, but rather as a broad conceptual model that you in conjunction with your security consultant can best enable you to actualize your security objectives.

The Protection Planning Process starts with an At Risk Assessment. This is where your security consultant evaluates your protection concerns and needs with you. Experience shows us that this phase of the process can take some time in order to drill down on the details to make certain all the bases are covered. High-quality security consultants will often bring up issues their high-net-worth clients have not previously thought about.

From here you go to Evaluating and Select Alternative Security Solutions. There are a variety of different kinds of threats and a large number of different types of security solutions to combat them. Add to these your unique circumstances and we have a plethora of combinations. In this phase, working with you, your security consultant will examine a number of different ways of ensuring the safety of what is important. As part of this phase conceptual algorithms are employed that help place security needs and particular security solutions in perspective.

Based on the evaluation, you in concert with your security consultant, select the security solutions. These solutions are deemed to be the best ones available taking into account a variety of factors such as their impact on your life and that of your loved ones, their cost and the time horizon involved.

Once your security consultant knows the security solutions you will be applying, he or she constructs the Action Plan. At this time, the selected security solutions are customized to your unique situation. Part of constructing the Action Plan is confirming your security needs. From Evaluating and Selecting Security Solutions to the Action Plan, it's not uncommon for life to change. Everything from burglaries and marital separations to unexpected overseas travel and missing medical records has prompted quick modifications to proposed Action Plans.

After knowing what to do — the Action Plan — your security consultant moves to doing — Implementation. There are some security solutions that require considerable ongoing involvement and commitment for you or others and some that operate in the background without much of your direct involvement once you have made the decision to move forward with them. Either way, this is where "things" happen.

Even after you have implemented the Action Plan, your security consultant will need to be constantly updating the security solutions you're employing. From situations changing in your world to changes in what is state-of-the-art in the private client protection field there will regularly be a call for tweaking to overhauling your Action Plan.

Why the Protection Planning Process Is So Effective

There are a lot of people holding themselves out as security consultants. More than a few of them are not doing much more than hawking one or another service such as providing security for large social events or installing an alarm system in a residence (see **Chapter 5: Caveat Emptor**). While these security consultants may very well be quite proficient at what they are doing, this is not the perspective the most of the leading authorities working with the wealthy are taking because it usually does not effectively meet their protection needs and concerns.

At the same time, there are a good number of exceptional security consultants who have the experience, sophistication and talent to efficaciously serve the wealthy. They are the professionals in the upper echelon of the private client security world. As we'll see in **Chapter 5: Caveat Emptor**, it's your responsibility to make certain you're working with one of these professionals as opposed to a pretender to the throne.

The Protection Planning Process is solution focused. It's focused on the well being of the entire family by providing security solutions specific to the risks associated with their lifestyles. More to the point, when security consultants who specialize in serving the wealthy are asked what they do, the answer is along the lines of: "We craft and implement security solutions for our private clients." They do not say they are bodyguards or asset protection planning specialists or describe any role that is inherently tied to a specific service or product. On the contrary, their role is to identify and solve your security problems. While, they may have areas where they are considered niche experts, they nonetheless, are adept at taking a holistic view of a wealthy individual's as well as his or her loved one's security situation. This problem solving orientation is inculcated into the Protection Planning Process.

Once your security consultant has identified and derived with your involvement the right security solutions, he or she acts as a principal contractor bringing together all the talents needed to effectively and meaningfully manage your protection concerns. And, as it often happens, especially when dealing with the more exotic protection needs of high-net-worth clients, your security consultant will regularly bring in niche experts.

Socrates maintained that he was an extremely ignorant man. He held this position despite his great knowledge — or more precisely because of it; he knew enough to understand how much he did not know. No matter how vast their expertise, the increasingly complicated nature of crafting security solutions for the financially well-to-do (moreover, for the ultra-affluent) is such that there will be occasions when your security consultants are not fully proficient on a security solution. At these times, it behooves them to turn to niche experts. The niche experts must "fill the gaps" in the skill sets and knowledge base of your security consultants.

Relatively few professionals in the security field are truly niche experts let alone capable of identifying and meeting the broad and intricate security needs of the wealthy. The greater majority tend to take an off-kilter snapshot of a client's security needs. Furthermore, what many security consultants do is find where their particular service fits in and then gear everything they do to getting that service sold (see **Chapter 5: Caveat Emptor**).

What differentiates the Protection Planning Process is the way it addresses the complete array of wealthy client security needs. As noted, it's a holistic approach to making certain you understand and evaluate the security needs of your world and make intelligent informed decisions as to how to manage those risks. At the very same time, the Protection Planning Process can be utilized to deal, laser like, with a specific security need.

Another way the Protection Planning Process differs from what so many security consultants do is that it's predicated on your involvement. It's imperative for every security consultant when working with high-net-worth clients that their clients offer their opinions, ask questions and share their ideas. When the wealthy constantly provide input they set an important precedent for the give-and-take between themselves and their security consultants. In such an environment, your security consultants are better able to suggest tentative security solutions promoting the eventual selection of the right security solutions which are then individualized appropriately.

Although many security consultants ask for opinions, feelings and feedback, we strongly feel that you should take the initiative. This perspective is integrated into the Protection Planning Process. Sometimes, for even the most adroit security consultants, it can be like pulling teeth to get a client to open up. Some of the wealthy are worried that their protection concerns make them appear less "important." Other members of the financial elite do not want to bother their security consultant about the "little things" that so often prove to be critical such as the movie producer who will not fly unless he is flying in the largest commercial jets in the world or the international business owner who ignored death threats against himself and his grandchildren because he did not think them credible as they came by email from inside one of his companies. As this is about you and protecting what is "valuable" to you, the Protection Planning Process was developed to warrant that YOU are at the center and remain there and that you're extensively involved. As such, your open input is a requisite.

There is another aspect about the Protection Planning Process that makes it as effective as it is. The Protection Planning Process is strongly educationally oriented. There is a well developed and refined pedagogical methodology incorporated into the process. It's our fervent belief that in every aspect of ensuring your well being and the well being of the people you care about requires you to make intelligent informed decisions and this is made possible by you becoming educated on what it takes to be safe and sound.

Some wealthy clients mistakenly believe that in hiring the security consultant they are now protected. It's not enough to hire a security consultant nor even implement an array of security solutions. We know all too well that these steps do not get you very far unless you're actively involved in the core aspects of planning as well as being involved in the execution of many of the security solutions. For many wealthy clients, this requires a change in mindset.

A case in point is that too many high-net worth individuals think by hiring close protection personnel, they can then do whatever they please and their "bodyguards" will take care of any problems that might arise. If you need to hire close protection personnel, then you also need to work intimately with them to mitigate the possibility of confrontations.

A final point of differentiation is that the Protection Planning Process draws upon the latest research and analysis in the field. By constantly evaluating the efficacy of various security solutions in the "real world" as well as in extensive simulations, leading security consultants are able to bring the latest and most effective security solutions to you. In other words, the Protection Planning Process was developed both "in the trenches" and in the "laboratory" resulting in a systematic proven methodology. In this way it can be compared to the best-in-class models derived in any industry as a result of benchmarking and quality process analysis.

To summarize, the Protection Planning Process is so powerful because of its focus and its design (Exhibit 3.1). It's a problem solving holistic approach that enables you to manage every or any aspect of security risk. It requires involvement on your part. This involvement is evidenced in the decision making as well as the educational orientation of the process. Because of your involvement, you and the people and things that you want to keep safe and sound are at the center point enabling your security consultants to provide the best solutions to keep them safe and sound. And, the Protection Planning Process is so robust because it's a "best practices" approach combining the most up-to-date simulations and empirical analyses in the field coupled with years upon years of hands-on experience.

Exhibit 3.1: What Makes the Personal Protection Process Effective

Problem solving orientation	• Not about specific protection strategies or tactics • Geared to delivering highly customized security solutions to high-net-worth clients
Holistic focus	• Can address the entire lifestyle and concerns of the high-net-worth individual and family • Can be laser focused on managing specific risks
High-net-worth client	• Education of the high-net-worth client is built into the process • Requires the high-net-worth client to understand the options in order to make well informed decisions
Based on best practices in the private client protection field	• Incorporates state-of-the-art empirically derived insights • Leverages years of experience in the trenches

Now, let's examine in greater detail the Protection Planning Process.

The At Risk Assessment

It's an impossibility to take the proper steps to be safe and sound until you know what is at risk — hence, the At Risk

Assessment. Assuming you want to address all the potential security risks you may confront — the holistic approach — this leads to a certain degree of intimacy between yourself and your security consultant. Your security consultant, in order to work with you to select and execute the proper security solutions, must know a great deal about your life, what you own and even what you see for yourself in the near term.

In conjunction with your security consultant you need to create a profile that details your life and those you care about in relation to protection concerns issues. The way we look at this is first from the perspective of the four protection concerns discussed in the previous chapter.

Guided Inquiry

The objective of the At Risk Assessment is to glean as much information as possible surrounding your life and those of your loved ones so as to ascertain the level of risk each person faces. To gather this information, leading security consultants employ a methodology know as guided inquiry.

Guided inquiry is a formal systematic way of using questions to gather information and do more. The philosophical foundation of guided inquiries dates back to Socrates. With respect to the various protection concerns, the following are some of the questions you will be asked:

Yourself and your loved ones

- How are the travel habits of you and your loved ones putting people at risk?
- Are all household staff members properly vetted prior to being retained?
- Who is "out to get you"?

- Have you ever done anything worthy of motivating blackmail?

- Where is your name recognized?

Your confidential information

- To what extent should your electronic communications be encrypted?

- Is your family trained to identify "pretext" calls?

- What levels of communication security are appropriate for your family members while on the telephone and computer?

- What electronic surveillance countermeasures have been implemented to ensure communication privacy?

- Have all credit bureaus been instructed not to provide personal information to anyone?

Your wealth

- To whom are you entrusting your monies?
    - Are the advisors reputable?
    - Do they have any skeletons in their closets?
    - What is their personal financial position?

- How trustworthy are your business associates?
    - Do they have any skeletons in their closets?
    - What is their personal financial position?

- Who knows how your assets are structured?
- What would happen if you're the victim of a frivolous lawsuit?
- What would happen if your child marries a gold digger, is divorced and is sued for egregious support?
- What if your child is in a car accident with your car?

Your property

- What level of access does the household staff have throughout the residence and property?
- What vendors are on site and have they been thoroughly investigated prior to being granted access?
- What levels of security from infrared border beam linked to the house alarm system to exterior lights are in place to identify intruders at the outer perimeter?
- Is there a safe haven? If so, where, equipped with what, built by whom, and what is the frequency of trial usage?
- What is the grid analysis for reported crimes surrounding the residence?

You will find, however, that the At Risk Assessment is much more than merely a data dump from you to your security consultant. At this level of professionalism, it's not merely about collecting facts. Many of the initial questions will center on obtaining information. But, there is much more to guided inquiries than just collecting an assortment of facts and preferences especially as you progress through the Protection Planning Process.

Other questions are used to test your understanding. In order to make intelligent and informed decisions any misconceptions concerning gauging the risks, as well as the requirements and responsibilities of various security solutions, requires that you truly understand the key issues. Proficient security consultants regularly employ questions that help you to interpret and compare options. Conceptually we're not dealing with rocket science (although some of the security solutions use the same technologies used by rocket scientists). Therefore, it's the responsibility of your security consultant to make sure you have a solid understanding of your situation and options to make informed intelligent decisions.

Along the same lines, your security consultant will use questions that require you to analyze and evaluate. For instance, in making informed decisions about various alternative security solutions, you will need to delve into the various possibilities — potential outcomes. A good way to facilitate thinking through this endeavor is with questions.

One of the attributes that makes the Protection Planning Process so effective is your involvement — the fact that you're educated to make intelligent informed decisions as well as actively participate in securing your own safety and that of those who are meaningful to you. The guided inquiry approach was developed to gather the requisite information but more importantly to place you at the center of the process and at the center of your protected future.

Who Participates in the Guided Inquiries

While questions are central to enabling your security consultant to develop a proper understanding of your situation and protection needs, the context of the questioning varies on a case-by-case basis. In some situations, the At Risk Assessment will be one-on-one between you and your security consultant. In other situations spouses are interviewed together — sometimes apart. At other times, the information will be solicited in a group environment: you, your spouse, other family members and one or more of your financial or legal advisors.

Occasionally, At Risk Assessments are conducted at a family offsite meeting. The rationale for the offsite is to have key members of the family available to identify protection concerns that impact them as well as generating consensus among family members with respect to potential security solutions. Experience demonstrates that with some large wealthy families, offsites meetings can be very powerful and that they can move the profiling process along expeditiously.

What you need to take into account is that in this phase of the process your security consultant needs to collect a considerable amount of information. We bring this to your attention because, surprisingly often, wealthy clients want their security consultants to take care of things and they do not even have a handle on what those things might be.

Once your security consultants have a firm grip at what is at risk, we move to the next phase in the process. However, before turning to the matter of security solutions, it's important to realize that very often leading security consultants are called in by the wealthy to conduct security audits — an in the "trenches" variation of an At Risk Assessment.

Security Audits

The greater majority of the wealthy have employed one kind or another of security consultant. A majority of them have also had negative — or, at a minimum, less than positive — experiences with security consultants (see **Chapter 5: Caveat Emptor**). As with every other professional specialty, there are those who can talk the talk but have some problem with walking. Unfortunately, with a fair number of dubious "security experts" soliciting business from the wealthy, security audits have become a significant growth component of the business.

Not only are the wealthy who are dissatisfied with their security consultants seeking security audits, but so are the wealthy who presently feel confident in the security solutions they have implemented. In the case of the latter, they desire to confirm they are doing the best that they can given their circumstances. In effect, can they enhance their zone of protection; can they readily pass the "mirror test?" A security audit ensures passing the "mirror test."

The concept of the security audit came into its own in the 1980s with the proliferation of "tiger teams." In the world of hackers we have the white hats and the black hats. The good guys — the white hats — comprise "tiger teams" whose objective is to break into the computer systems of a company where the company hired them to do so. The company's objective is to test their computer security.

This concept commuted to protecting the wealthy where security consultants are called upon to probe and sometimes penetrate the security defenses of a high-net-worth client. Increasingly we see high-net-worth clients attracted to the idea of testing their defenses. In fact, about a quarter (24.6%) of the wealthy we surveyed had conducted some form of security audit (Exhibit 3.2). Nearly half the ultra-affluent (48.1%), a little more that a fifth of the affluent (21.8%) and slightly less than a fifth of the low-end affluent (17.5%) had conducted security audits.

Security audits cover a surfeit of different actions. Some security audits are fairly benign and straightforward. This is exemplified by the affluent client who hires a security consultant to make recommendations concerning the alarm system he installed in his house. On the other end of the spectrum is the high-net-worth client who hired a security consultant to break into his house (which he claimed had an undefeatable state-of-the-art security system) and place a box of chocolates next to his prized $7 million painting. After successfully broaching the house's defenses and leaving the chocolate, the security consultant was hired to make sure – on an ongoing basis, that – the loved ones, personal information and property of his new ultra-affluent client was safe and sound.

Exhibit 3.2: Conducted a Security Audit

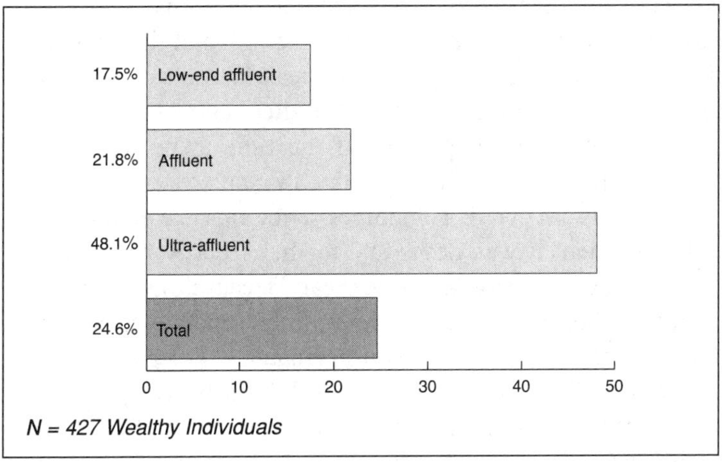

What proves to be more to the point is that 76.2 percent of the wealthy who conducted a security audit found that their security could be improved (Exhibit 3.3). A slightly greater percentage of the low-end affluent (83.3%) found gaps in their protection compared to 71.0 percent for the affluent and 73.7 percent for the ultra-affluent.

Exhibit 3.3: Security Audits Identify Opportunities for Improvement

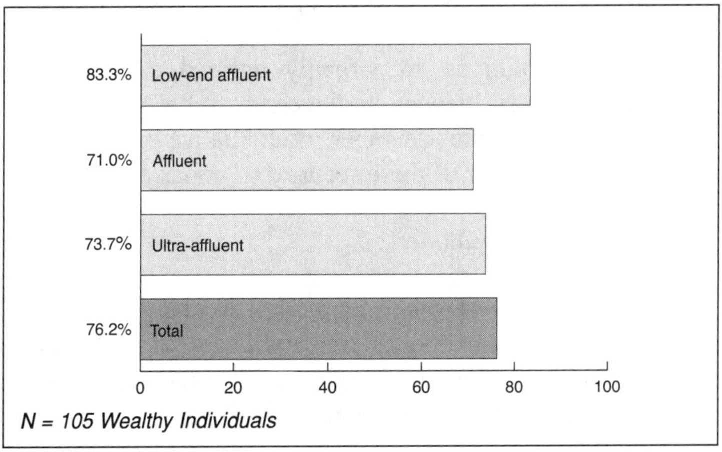

Our experience in conducting security audits says that very few high-net-worth individuals cannot be made safer. This also goes for their loved ones, their wealth and their property. Even when they are using the services of a security consultant the consensus in the industry is that after conducting a security audit about 70 to 80 percent of the time there are ways to enhance the security of the wealthy. In many cases only a little tweaking is involved; sometimes a lot more. For one ultra-affluent client it was necessary for his security consultant to oversee the armoring of his new car. Because of the level and scope of the risks the client opted to incorporate remote controlled sirens, tear gas and flash grenades. For another high-net-worth client, her security consultant selectively scrubbed her identity meaning all personal information about her and her immediate family was legally taken out of the public domain.

Evaluating Alternative Security Solutions

With your At Risk Assessment in hand the next step is to consider the various security solutions you can use to mitigate your protection risks. There are a great many different security methodologies and technologies you can employ. Meanwhile the elasticity of the practice of providing security solutions for the wealthy means that no set of procedures, no scripts, no packaged answers are possible; everything must be customized.

Security solutions are broadly defined categories of "answers" to a security need. In the context of each protection concern there are quite a number of alternative security solutions. A few examples of these security solutions are:

Yourself and you loved ones

- *Crisis contingency planning.* Wealthy clients and selected loved ones are provided with professional security training. Education can often prove instrumental in reducing the risk of being involved in a crisis. This is accomplished in a number of ways all predicated on simulation exercises. At one end of the spectrum we have individual or small group working discussion sessions. At the other end of the spectrum we have intense role play scenarios.

- *Close protection services.* Close protection personnel come in all types and combinations from petite unassuming individuals to large teams. It all depends of the circumstances. However, close protection is much more than having defensive personnel at attention. High quality close protection includes extensive advanced work and reconnaissance, examining vehicles and buildings to be used by the high-net-worth client, preparing emergency evacuation routes and liaising with police and security organizations when appropriate.

- *Transporter services.* This is a version of close protection when a wealthy family needs to have loved ones chaperoned in and out of locations. With the problems surrounding the Middle East, for example, transporter services were provided to the children of a wealth family as well as their friends and teachers who were "stuck" in Egypt weeks before the onset of the second Gulf War.

- *Extensive background and periodic ongoing assessments of employees.* We saw examples of unscrupulous employees in the very beginning of the book – the nanny, the personal assistant and the gardener (see **How To Use This Book**). All too often the weak link in a wealthy person's security is someone on the "inside." Therefore, not only should background assessments be conducted when a person is hired, it's wise to from time to time conduct personnel assessments.

Your confidential information

- *Education on keeping secrets secret.* A great deal of confidential information is handed over or made easily available to other people on a regular basis. Many of the wealthy, for instance, have a paper shredder at their offices but they do not have a paper shredder at their homes. At their homes they simply place all sorts of documents such as bills and receipts into the garbage – that is easily available to any dumpster diver. Sometimes, confidential information is requested by a criminal and then handed over as in the case of computer passwords. There is always some pretext given for needing the password, and a wily criminal knows which ones work well when. Learning about these ploys is a good first step to keepings secrets secret.

- *Identity assessments and checks.* For many wealthy people, it makes sense to presume that their identities have been stolen. Then it's just a matter of checking commercially available (and sometimes select proprietary) data bases to see if a high-net-worth client has done or is doing anything he or she would not have. If something turns up, as is periodically the case, then corrective action can be taken quickly. Otherwise, there is a high probability of considerably more damage being inflicted.

- *Counter-surveillance services.* When it would be disastrous for personal or business conversations to be known to certain other people, it's an intelligent move to sweep locations for surveillance equipment. Moreover, at these times it's also very beneficial to make sure no one can listen in over long distances such as into your living room while you're speaking with your attorney.

- *Encryption services.* It's exceedingly easy to steal information when that information is in transit. From cell phones to email, there are a variety of strategies enabling criminals to share in the messages. When it's important that this information remain confidential, the wealthy can turn to a menu of encryption services to make certain only the people they want to have the information have it.

Your wealth

- *Extensive background reviews of financial and professional advisors.* With financial fraud a growth industry and the wealthy a prime target, making sure that the advisor you're entrusting monies to is indeed trustworthy tends to be a smart move. It's quite often the case that an unscrupulous advisor has been plying his or her nefarious trade for some time. A little digging can save a lot of money let alone the amount of anxiety and aggravation that can be avoided.

- *Investigations of potential business partners.* As with financial and professional advisors, it's often prudent to make sure a person you would be going into business with will not end up taking advantage of you. While you will never know for certain, by being cognizant of his or her professional history you can get a good "feel" for the likelihood or possibility that you can be a target.

- *Second opinions on proposed financial transactions.* Even when the people you're doing business with are credible and have integrity, that does not mean they are making intelligent financial recommendations. Just consider all the — what are now clearly — abusive tax strategies that have been marketed to the wealthy over the last five plus years. Even with the Internal Revenue

Service scrutinizing more and more tax strategies, there is still a legion of advisors promoting hyper-aggressive questionably legal tax strategies. Hence, many wealthy individuals when seriously considering a more aggressive tax strategy are increasingly obtaining second opinions on their merits.

- *Asset protection strategies.* There is a broad array of potential asset protection strategies that the wealthy can employ to create a legal fortress around their wealth keeping creditors and litigants out while enabling them to move their wealth freely in and out of the fortress. Examples of these strategies include various corporate structures, spendthrift and self-settled trusts, equity stripping and the adroit use of structured products.

Your property

- *Detailed access protocols.* All too often, with respect to larger estates, people seem to come and go as they please. From FedEx deliveries to the landscaping service and from repair people to the parents of your children's friends, there is easy access to the property. It's logical to be put in place access protocols that set the parameters as to who can and cannot be on the grounds as well as in the house as well as when they can and cannot.

- *Safe havens.* Often in conjunction with architectural firms safe havens are installed in residences and mega yachts. Safe havens can be designed and constructed at various levels of security predicated on your At Risk Assessment. At the low end, they can be rooms reinforced and impregnated with ballistic materials. Moving to the high end, they can be constructed ensuring complete protection from access from outside the room incorporating closed circuit television, air conditioning and filtration systems as well as stored oxygen, extensive amounts of food and survival supplies and multiple communication systems.

- *Surveillance and alarm systems.* Today, there is the opportunity to install highly sophisticated alarm and surveillance systems on the property. Closed circuit television cameras, for example, are becoming the norm and can be installed literally anywhere. It's becoming increasingly common to place such cameras not only to observe the perimeter of the residence but within the communal spaces of the residence (e.g., the formal dinning room, the living room, the gallery). This way when the wealthy family is traveling, they can observe the state of their house using their portable computer or personal digital assistant.

- *Transporter services.* We previously addressed transporter services with respect to people. Their more common use is for property. One ultra-affluent client uses transporter services to move her jewelry from her safe deposit boxes to her possession and back again. Another ultra-affluent client uses such services for both business and family legal documents. A third ultra-affluent client has close protection for his Arabian horses when they are in transit.

What makes the matter even more complicated is the fact that the private client protection industry is extremely fast moving. When looking over the last decade, you see the pace of evolution is exponential, driven by technological advances as well as a need to adapt to much more complex lifestyles of low-end affluent, the affluent and ultra-affluent combined with a justifiably scarier world. This translates into the continuous development of new security solutions (Exhibit 3.4).

Exhibit 3.4: Future Security Solutions

Yourself and your loved ones	• Satellite based tracking of loved ones • Completely customized insurance policies tightly integrated with the Protection Planning Process and the Crisis Intervention Process
Your confidential information	• Use of data havens • Personalized encryption keys
Your wealth	• Transforming real property into securities and then "hedging" it • Derivative based strategies to legally circumvent the Uniform Fraudulent Transfer Act as it's currently written
Your property	• Residences that fight back • Biometric smart cards

In the near future, you will be able — if you so choose — to track, by satellite, loved ones wherever they are in the world. Early adopters are likely to be international travelers and very concerned parents.

Today, you can purchase insurance and, to a limited degree, the services of a security consultant are tied in. Around the corner, the wealthy will be able to construct a policy which will be designed to their unique needs and wants. Critical to this will be the fact that these policies will not be any more expensive than existing policies but will incorporate significantly more protection elements as well as crisis intervention elements.

Just as there are tax havens throughout the world, we're on the brink of data havens. They will provide the ultimate in information privacy as you use the Internet. Along similar lines, the financial elite as well as the corporate elite will have their own personalized encryption keys enabling them to communicate with conventional communication technology and be assured their communications are private.

Today, where the Homestead Act does not exist, equity stripping is one of the best ways to make real property judgment proof. In the foreseeable future, it will be possible to metamorphasize real estate into a "stock." Subsequently, you would be able to "hedge" the "stock" with the effect of making it disappear as an asset in your estate. This methodology would permit you to live in a mansion with the mansion not existing as part of your portfolio of assets and thereby be completely protected from creditors and the like.

Moving a little farther down our future time line, there are likely to be derivative transactions that would circumvent the Uniform Fraudulent Transfer Act as it's *currently written.* Provided there is no change in the Act, this would enable you, even after a judgment against you, to move assets out of your estate thereby protecting them from existing judgments yet still maintain control over them.

When it comes to your property such as your home, the security systems are almost always designed to keep criminals out and "sound the alarm" if they penetrate the residence. At hand, and soon to be democratized, is technology that fights back against an intruder. Houses will be equipped with the likes of tasers, tear gas, flash grenades, impact netting as well as lethal and non-lethal shotgun weaponry. The house will actually attack the intruder.

An interrelated evolution will be smart cards attuned only to you and selected others that will enable you to operate the defenses of the hi-tech house or boat. For example, it will provide the means of obtaining entrance and egress to your property. In effect, you will have extensively more control over who can get in or out.

The technology and processes for these security solutions exist today. However, many are still prototypes. In time, we're likely to see these security solutions become part and parcel of the alternatives that the wealthy will be considering.

Selecting Security Solutions

The way this phase of the Protection Planning Process usually works is that your security consultants will speedily narrow down the gamut of security solutions and their multitude of variations to a workable number. Then in conjunction with you, they will select the most viable ones for your particular situation.

In order to select the appropriate security solutions in conjunction with your security consultant, you would consider a number of "What ifs." For example:

- *What if* someone kidnapped your daughter?
- *What if* you're being followed everywhere by an obsessive fan?
- *What if* someone is listening in on all your phone calls and is reading all your emails?
- *What if* a stranger knows how much money you have and where it all is?
- *What if* someone steals your identity and empties all your accounts?
- *What if* someone filed a frivolous but very real lawsuit against you for $50 million?
- *What if* you invested $2 million with a hedge fund manager who actually is not managing any money?
- *What if* someone broke into your house?
- *What if* when you got on board your private plan you found it trashed?

As we discussed in **Chapter 1: Are Your Safe?,** the odds are certainly in your favor. There is a very low probability that your child or grandchild will be abducted, just as there is a very low probability that your phone will be tapped or that you will be the victim of a large frivolous lawsuit or the mark of a brilliantly calculating con artist.

To gain better perspective on the need for a security solution to handle a protection need leading security consultants use the following conceptual algorithm:

Need for a Security Solution = Probability of Incident x Severity of Incident

What top security consultants end up doing is helping their high-net-worth clients think through the likelihood of a security problem in the context of what it means to them if it did indeed happen. For example, let us say you live in a very safe neighborhood as confirmed by a grid analysis for reported crimes surrounding the residence and you have already taken a lot of wise steps to protect your house.

Objectively, we can conclude that the probability of someone breaking in and stealing something is very low. For a few wealthy clients, having their house robbed is an inconvenience – a major inconvenience, but an inconvenience nonetheless. For these high-net-worth clients, a security consultant will usually determine that additional home security systems are often unnecessary. In contrast, there are high-net-worth clients for whom the very idea of someone breaking into their house literally gives them the shakes; makes them physically ill. They see it as a great personal violation to be avoided at all costs. For these wealthy clients there is a need to significantly and often dramatically enhance the security systems in the homes. Obviously, most people fall in the middle of these two extremes.

With most incidents there is a very low probability of anything happening. You're not likely to be mugged or to have someone break into your house while you're out-of-town and your family is at home nor is it likely that your babysitter will sexually assault your children. The odds for everything that can go bad are quite low. The real determinant of the need to provide a security solution for a particular protection concern is how you will react, how you will feel if the incident did indeed happen; remember the "mirror test" (see **Chapter 1: Are You Safe?).**

It's useful to think of security solutions as insurance policies. It's best when they are not used, but critical if they need to be used. A central difference between an insurance policy and a security solution is that there are times the security solution can also act as a deterrent. Having closed circuit television cameras strategically positioned on your house will likely make burglars look for less well protected fare.

It's imperative to remember the criminal mantra of negative migration. Negative migration is where criminal behavior migrates to the path of least resistance. Consequently, criminals are more inclined to look for the easiest target all things considered. It's therefore possible to leverage the concept of negative migration. So, the burglar will likely choose a house where the security is not as extensive.

Having decided that there is a protection need, the matter turns to which security solution. As we have noted, there are a tremendous number of such solutions. What quality security consultants will do is narrow down this multitude of possibilities to a workable number. They draw on their experiences with an eye to industry best practices. With a manageable number of security solutions, they employ another conceptual algorithm — the net value of a security solution.

$$\textbf{Net Value of a Security Solution} = \frac{\textbf{Intensity x Duration}}{\textbf{Lifestyle Considerations x Financial Considerations}}$$

Every security solution has four variables that can be modified within set parameters. One is intensity. How concentrated should the security solution be? To avoid someone listening in to your phone calls you can have a niche expert periodically sweep the phone lines for bugs or you can increase the intensity by deploying phone encryption equipment.

Another valuable is duration. How long will the security solution be active? Consider a close protection team. If you're traveling to parts of the world where kidnapping is a business proposition you might want this security solution when you do. On the other hand, this may very well be overkill when you're at home or office.

These two variables are the numerators of our conceptual algorithm. The denominators are lifestyle considerations and financial considerations. Lifestyle considerations are the extent to which a security solution is an impediment to your lifestyle. For instance, having a close protection team with you wherever you go may be intrusive to the point it proves counterproductive.

Financial considerations are the costs of using a particular security solution. You might want to make sure your house is safe. On the one hand, you can put in a first rate conventional alarm system. On the other hand, you can spend a great deal more by including thermal sensors, internal and external cameras, a safe haven, infrared trip wires and so forth. The difference in cost is considerable and therefore needs to be taken into account.

The Action Plan

Once your security consultants have, with your direction, selected the various security solutions that will potentially work best, all things considered, they now need to formally specify everything that needs to be done. This phase of the

Protection Planning Process is where you're provided with a detailed accounting of what is to be done to ensure the security with respect to each of the four protection concerns. This is when the "game plan" is made very clear.

For your security consultant a component of this phase of the process entails reviewing with you your At Risk Assessment. It's imperative that everyone involved from you and your spouse to children and the appropriate professional advisors such as your attorneys have a common understanding of what you want accomplished and how your objectives (i.e., the application of various security solutions) achieves your protection objectives. While your security consultants are always soliciting feedback from you, this is the time when that solicitation process is most intently focused and exhaustive.

A skilled security consultant will make extreme efforts to make certain there have been no miscommunications and that all parties are on the same page. And, if there have been miscommunications that they are corrected quickly.

During the review of where you are and where you want to be, any meaningful digression from the core premises and assumptions derived from the information you have provided is a red flag. Many times the genesis of red flags is very recent changes in what is happening in your life. One ultra-affluent client was not interested in a very intense application of certain security solutions until an incident at one of his homes. After the break-in, he decided that a major upgrading of the security systems at all his various houses was in order.

When a red flag goes up, your security consultant must make sure that your situation and preferences have been accurately profiled and updated. Sometimes red flags go up because a wealthy client is not initially comfortable enough to divulge certain facts that are crucial to ensuring he or she feels secure. Some examples that fit into this category include the existence of concubines, hesitations concerning the self-efficacy of children as well as their choices of friends and associates and how really scared they are.

The Action Plan is a document detailing all the security solutions that will be used. It also sets the timeline for implementation.

Implementation

The most straightforward part of the Protection Planning Process is implementation. This does not mean implementation is easy — it always calls for a tremendous amount of work including work on your part. While customization of security solutions is the norm, your security consultants are on very familiar ground and enacting the various security solutions is something all high-quality security consultants do extremely well as the key skill sets in implementation are diligence and precision.

Just as there are red flags when it comes to the Action Plan, there are changes that can derail the Protection Planning Process and make Implementation of the chosen security solutions inappropriate. Such changes, a real threat to your children for example, are analogous to either the bride or groom going AWOL at the grand wedding because they bring the proceedings — and Implementation — to a grinding halt. If there is nothing to derail the Action Plan, it's time to take action.

Another aspect of Implementation is to ensure you're in-synch with what was confirmed in the Action Plan. At this time, your security consultant will:

- *Re-confirm your At Risk Assessment.* Once again, it's crucial to ensure that the information upon which the Action Plan was developed and implemented is accurate.

- *Re-confirm the desired results.* High-quality security consultants are always asking themselves: "Are you getting what you expect and are paying for?" This is one of the times they make an even greater effort to make sure that the Action Plan meets your protection objectives and goals.

- *Re-confirm everyone's responsibilities.* Your security consultant clearly has responsibilities when it comes to Implementation and so do you. You must be aware of what your role must be.

Follow Through

Both the empirical studies we conducted over the years and our personal observations of the field confirm the persistence of a critical mistake made by many security consultants and their clients after Implementation. Relatively few security consultants do a stellar, or even an adequate job of following through. It's not that uncommon for there to be no follow through at all.

The Action Plan has been implemented and nothing is going wrong – so far. The wealthy client has an individualized crisis intervention plan, for instance, or a new alarm system for her yacht. Leading security consultants find it's imperative to continually stay abreast of the various changes that require re-examining which security solutions are optimal. Follow through comes in three forms: environmental scanning, high-net-worth client driven contact and ongoing or periodic reviews.

Environmental scanning. We touched on the breakneck pace of change in the private client protections field. Some of these changes are due to the changing technological environment. Other changes are a product of geopolitics. Some changes are due to other environmental alterations that are local. Your security consultant will keep on top of all these changes with you in mind. As these changes occur, your security consultant will need to determine how these changes impact your personal situation and when to bring them to your attention.

From time to time there is also the necessity for a more formal updating of your At Risk Assessment. The recommendation of a new security solution or the modification of an existing one is predicated on the accuracy of this assessment so, as circumstances frequently change, regular updating of your situation will enable your security consultant to evaluate whether a new or enhanced version of a security solution fits best.

High-net-worth client driven contact. There are many times when you or one of your financial or legal advisors will contact your security consultant because of changes in your life. Anything that impacts your world in a meaningful way such as marriages, job changes, or changes in residences should prompt a reconnection. When this occurs, there is a need to update your profile and then proceed through the various phases of the Protection Planning Process once again.

Ongoing and periodic reviews. Due to the nature of making you safe and sound, it's a given that you will need to intermittently meet with your security consultant and other key people in your world to ensure everything is going in the right direction, that all the moving parts of a security solution(s) are working smoothly in concert.

With a relatively small number of security solutions, there is extensive and continuous contact between your security consultant and you and/or your advisors. Take for example the use of close protection personnel. This ongoing contact results in ongoing reviews.

It's All About People

While high-quality security consultants can bring to the table the most sophisticated thinking and competencies in the field of private client protection, it's a mistake to place too much emphasis on the technical and methodological wizardry involved. As opposed to what game theory would tell us, human dynamics are more important to the Protection Planning Process than technical know-how. For all the wiz bang technology, for all the simulations and modeling your security consultant can conceptualize and run, success is predicated on being acutely attuned to the very human side of the world of the wealthy client.

Because it's all about people, a wealthy family can never be guaranteed to be protected against ever security risk. All the preparation, all the education, all the right moves will not assuredly stop a capable, motivated (or blindingly lucky) criminal. So, when things go wrong, what do you do? How should you handle a crisis? This is the topic of the next chapter.

Chapter 4

The Crisis Intervention Process

What would you do if someone broke into your home and you were not there but your family was?

What would you do if your 6 year old grandchild did not return home from school one day?

What would you do if someone did a "Godfather"—cut off your horse's head and left it in your bed for you to find?

What would you do if an ex-employee vows vengeance for some imagined slight and has already threatened your wife via email?

What would you do if you're told by an anonymous voice on the phone to look at a web site where you see pictures of your 14 year old daughter getting dressed in her room?

What often motivates the wealthy to seek out the services of security consultants is a crisis. A "disaster" ensues and there is the need for immediate action. There is a very effective crisis intervention process — developed for the wealthy — that is the exceptionally effective in managing these situations.

To better understand the Crisis Intervention Process, let us consider situations where it became necessary to implement the process.

Crisis Situation #1: The Disappearing Son

A very successful, highly opinionated and very vocal businessman found himself desperately searching for his six year old son once he was discovered missing from the grounds of his private school. When returning home several hours later unharmed, his son produced a note that plainly advised the businessman to "take caution" on his public views.

The addition of limited close protection coupled with enhanced protective measures for the house and business quickly contained the situation. A thorough review of all the employees at the private school identified a disaffected maintenance worker. This information was passed on to the police and the maintenance worker ended up confessing to the crime.

Crisis Situation #2: The Scared Sophomore

While attending her sophomore year at a one of the Seven Sisters, the daughter of an ultra-affluent family began to receive disturbing to even threatening calls. This was soon followed by non-threatening but harassing notes left under her door. Shortly thereafter, the daughter's father received an email at his place of business with pictures of his daughter at school and captions under the pictures requesting $500,000. Being that the statements were not accompanied by an "or else" or extortion statement, no law enforcement agency could take action.

Days later, the daughter left school after returning to her room and finding her dog hanging from the ceiling fan with a note stating: "You're next." The sophomore called up her parents in tears, telling them she was too frightened to leave her locked room.

Within hours specialists escorted the daughter from the college to the family's private jet. She was delivered to her family unharmed and very scared. Tracing the criminal through the emails sent to the father was not happening. On the other hand, a thorough investigation of all the people who had access to the daughter's room — one way or another — provided the leads. Within weeks, an ex-boyfriend was arrested.

Crisis Situation #3: Off to Join a Cult

A 16 year old decided to leave high school and leave his family in favor of a new religious movement. The girlfriend of the 16 year old was already a member of the group and was instrumental in the minor's deciding to run away. The religious group sees the current Mid East crisis as the telling sign of the end of the world. According to the leader of the cult, only by dedicating oneself to the true way and abandoning the evil paths people are now pursuing will they find salvation.

When he ran away, the 16 year old took nearly $300,000 out of the family household account with him.

It took almost three months to track down the location of the minor. In accordance with the law, a team of specialists extracted the minor from the situation. He was returned to his family and he went into counseling.

While the search for the minor was underway, the security surrounding the family was enhanced because of the death threats that they received from people believed to be members of the cult. Included here were the use of close protection, transporter services and enhanced security for residences and other property.

At the same time, investigators collected extensive information on the ex-girlfriend, the cult and its leader. This information is now being used in a multi-million dollar lawsuit against them. The investigators were able to obtain the evidence to prove that the leader of the cult personally directed all recruitment activities and were targeting minors fitting a specific profile.

Presently, the cult leader and a number of his followers are in prison awaiting trail. The family is maintaining a high level of security around themselves out of concern for fanatical cult members not incarcerated.

Crisis Situation #4: The Kidnapped Grandchild

He was in Venezuela doing field research on his doctoral dissertation when he was abducted. He was riding in a car with two other students. The car stopped when two men pointed machine pistols at them. The students stepped out of the car and a hood was placed over the head of the one from the affluent family. The other two students were roughed up. The ransom note requesting $10 million for the student's safe return was delivered to the United States embassy the next day.

The kidnappers knew who to take and how much to ask for. Negotiators were sent in and the kidnappers were paid off to the tune of $3 million and the hostage was safely returned.

Crisis Situation #5: The Potentially Costly Purchase

While in the midst of acquiring a competitor, a wealthy businessman developed a "gut feel" that critical information concerning his company, his negotiating strategy and his intentions were known by the managers of the other firm. He was always being placed in a "one-down" position during the negotiations and it looked like this would be a very costly purchase; but even so, he really wanted the acquisition to go through.

A review of the way confidential business information was handled uncovered a number of microphones serendipitously placed in offices, including the businessman's lawyer's office as well as in his private study at his house. All the "bugs" were removed and significant counter-surveillance procedures were put in place.

An extensive investigation determined that the source of the microphones was a part-time worker for the cleaning service the businessman uses at his business and his house. By the time the person was identified, he had disappeared.

Considering the integrity of management of the competitor, the businessman called off the deal. Because of the evidence the investigators collected, the businessman did not have to pay any penalties for discontinuing with the merger.

These are a few of the cases that have prompted the wealthy to enlist the services of security consultants. In all these situations and many more like them, after these kinds of experiences, the wealthy will usually go through the Protection Planning Process. It often takes something to go wrong or, worse yet, something to go terribly wrong before some of the financial elite become proactive.

Closing the Barn Door After the Horse Has Left

While the wealthy are clearly concerned (see **Chapter 1: Are You Safe?** and **Chapter 2: The Protection Concerns of the Wealthy),** there are many, even most, who are not concerned enough to take preemptive actions. Only 16.6 percent have crafted a crisis intervention plan of one sort or another (Exhibit 4.1). A quarter of the ultra-affluent (25.3%) have done so; proportionately fewer of the affluent (16.2%) and relatively fewer still of the low-end affluent (13.6%).

Exhibit 4.1: Currently Have a Crisis Intervention Plan

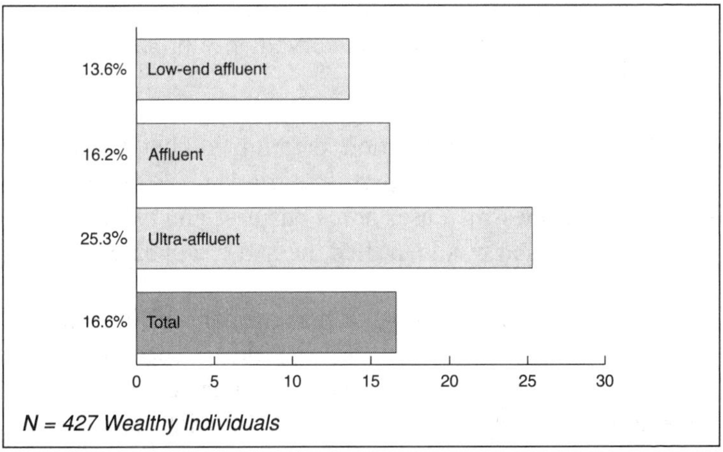

What also proves insightful is that of the 71 wealthy individuals who do indeed have some sort of crisis intervention plan, only 5.6 percent of them have reviewed the plan with a security consultant within the past year (Exhibit 4.2). None of the low-end affluent, only 8.7 percent of the affluent and 10.0 percent of the ultra-affluent are keeping their crisis intervention plans current.

Exhibit 4.2: Reviewed Their Crisis Intervention Plan within the Last Year

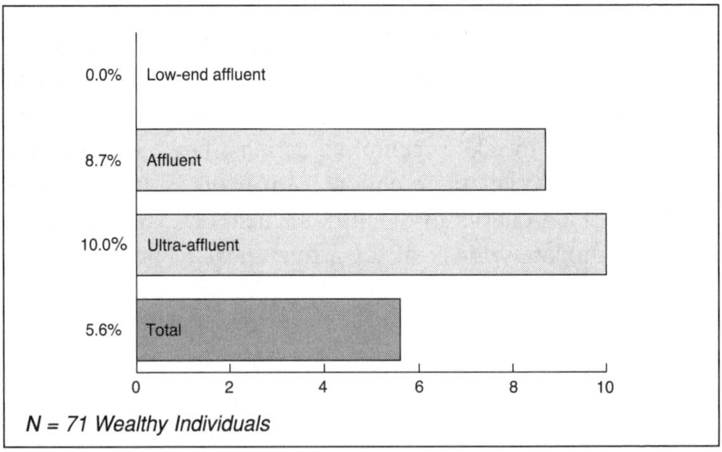

What is also very telling is that (and we'll review these findings in **Chapter 5: Caveat Emptor)** three quarters of the wealthy have hired security consultants in the last three years (although most are unhappy with them). Bottom-line: it often takes a deleterious incident to motivate some high-net-worth individuals to get focused when it comes to protecting themselves and what is important to them.

While security consultants are seeing more of the wealthy being proactive, this is principally a function of their professional advisors (e.g., their attorneys), prompting them to critically examine their protection needs as well as the security solutions they have implemented. Nevertheless, the greater majority of professional advisors are only directing their high-net-worth clients to security consultants when those clients explicitly request the service. The Latin American high-net-worth clients of one law firm were barraging them for recommendations for security consultants. After six months of such requests, the law firm took the steps to identify a security consulting firm to recommend to their clients. While there are numerous exceptions, the wealthy generally tend to turn to their professional advisors ranging from their attorneys and accountants to their bankers and financial advisors requesting the services of a security consultant when they are confronting a crisis.

On the other hand, a rapidly growing trend is for these professional advisors to be proactive as they often have a deep understanding of the particular situations of their high-net-worth clients and recognize that these clients would be well served by examining their protection concerns and the security solutions they have implemented to date. The more forward thinking professional advisors are taking the lead in the process by acting as overseers to ensure their wealthy clients are optimally benefited.

Many of the wealthy will take action to close the barn door after the horse has left – and this is smart. After a crisis has been resolved, without taking proactive steps, more adverse situations will almost assuredly happen to the financially successful family. This phenomenon is referred to as inverse negative migration. In other words, a lack of broad based action following a crisis is often followed by further crises. Hence, it's wise to forcefully close the barn door after the horse has left because otherwise there are more horses in the barn which might also get loose. So, we now turn to the Crisis Intervention Process.

The Crisis Intervention Process

When you progress through the Protection Planning Process, included is the crafting of a crisis intervention plan; this way you know how to respond when facing a security crisis. Whether a wealthy individual has a crisis intervention plan in place or not, when experienced security consultants are called in, they employ one version or another of the Crisis Intervention Process. Conceptually similar to the Protection Planning Process, the Crisis Intervention Process is composed of six phases: – (1) Triage; (2) Crisis Containment; (3) Crisis Assessment; (4) the Action Plan; (5) Implementation; and (6) Follow Through.

The first phase is Triage. Here the security consultants expeditiously conduct an evaluation of the situation and sequentialize threats and criminal activities. They then prioritize actions which brings us to the next phase — Crisis Containment. At this time a menu of precisely calculated actions are taken to deal with the immediate situation. There is a feedback loop from Crisis Containment to Triage. If the situation cannot be brought rapidly under control (which includes setting the foundation for further interventions), then it becomes necessary to reevaluate the crisis situation.

Because these two phases occur at a breakneck pace they are generally indistinguishable as separate phases. However, conceptually and operationally, they most certainly are.

With the immediate situation being appropriately dealt with, we turn to the Crisis Assessment. This is a much more involved evaluation of the situation. No longer are your security consultants just concerned with the presenting problems, but genesis issues are sought and multiplicative implications are discerned.

The security consultants then move from the assessment to putting together an Action Plan. Here is detailed the strategies and tactics that will be executed bringing you to the final phase, Implementation. There is a feedback loop from Implementation to Crisis Assessment. If progress is not being made in Implementation, your security consultants will need to return to Crisis Assessment and reexamine assumptions, facts and hypotheses.

Finally, we have Follow Through. Even when everything works out well — the crisis is managed and everyone and everything is safe and sound — there is still Follow Through. There are two basic components to Follow Through. One is to mitigate the risk of future security problems. As we noted, the horse has left the barn so it's time to close the barn door so no other horses get loose. It's not uncommon for high-net-worth clients of the Crisis Intervention Process, once the crisis is abrogated, to work through the Protection Planning Process.

The other component of Follow Through, involves psychological counseling. People change, sometimes very dramatically, after a security crisis. Consider the wealthy parents of a child who has been abducted. The child is recovered unharmed about a week later. In their own ways, the parents and the child are scared to be out of each other's sight. What is required aside from making sure the family is protected is to take action to ensure they can function effectively.

Everything from feelings of being violated — psychologically or physically -- to deprogramming to helping victims deal with their behavior produced by the Stockholm syndrome, requires specially trained and experienced counselors. In fact, psychological counseling to help victims deal with their reactions and feelings, their anxieties and the ongoing stress is a specialty. There are even a handful of counselors who specialize within this specialty; for example there are counselors who only work with workplace violence situations or the one who only works with stalking victims or the one who limits her work to children who were rescued from kidnappers. What is important is to recognize that there are often times after a crisis when professional psychological counseling support is strongly advised and that the Crisis Intervention Process was designed with this in mind.

In a Crisis, Speed is Often of the Essence

With rare exceptions, the faster constructive action is taken the better off you will be. Time is almost always on the side of the criminal.

As noted, high-quality security consultants, as part of the Protection Planning Process will develop a crisis intervention plan for their high-net-worth clients. In effect, when something goes wrong, the wealthy will know what to do immediately, short-term and longer-term. The crisis intervention plan, because it is predicated on extensive scenario modeling, enables the high-net-worth individual to react more expeditiously and more precisely.

Part of every crisis intervention plan is the 24-hour manned crisis management center. Thus, the wealthy are provided with immediate advice and assistance worldwide. Any security crisis hotline must serve a number of functions. Aside from getting you in touch with your security consultant when circumstances are more extreme, the hotline also helps you deal with non-urgent and routine enquiries immediately.

Going on Offense

One component of the Crisis Intervention Process is parochially known as "*going on offense.*" Sometimes, the investigative and related skills and talents of security consultants are employed to help remediate a problem situation. Going on offense is many times a viable and attractive option and it therefore becomes an integral part of the Action Plan. Because of the manner in which this preference benefits the wealthy, we need to spend a little time detailing it.

Conceptually, going on offense involves being highly proactive in working to remedy a security problem that occurred. The degree of "offense" is quite extensive from collecting information directly and/or unobtrusively that can bolster a legal case to tracking and recovering stolen assets to literally taking out the big guns which is exemplified when a security consultant facilitates the mounting of an operation using the services of elite ex-special forces personnel.

With respect to employing investigative expertise, there are two areas where leading security consultants find a great deal of high-net-worth client demand. One is asset searches and recovery initiatives and the other is litigation support. In the former, the security consultant is dealing with the loss of wealth and property often requiring the application of forensic accounting expertise coupled with other investigative talents.

Let us take a look at a three year hunt for missing assets that begins and ends in New York City with stops in the Cayman Islands, Switzerland, Italy, Greece, the Bahamas and Lichtenstein. Take one secretive ultra-affluent family whose wealth is calculated in the billions. They hail from the Middle East. Add one very polished con artist running a phenomenally successful — at least on paper- – investment firm and we have the major ingredients for a first-rate scam.

The ultra-affluent family, on the recommendation of a very close friend of the family who was educated in the United States and possesses an MBA from one of the top business schools, entrusted $15 million to the investment firm. While the investment firm was domiciled offshore, the initial meeting was held in a restaurant in New York City. In attendance were two members of the wealthy family, the president of the investment firm and the friend of the family who was making the introduction.

The president of the investment firm "guaranteed" that his firm doubles the money of their clients within two to three years. This claim was backed up by the friend of the family, who made the introduction and was paid by the ultra-affluent family to conduct the due diligence on the investment firm.

The investment firm's approach to money management was based on a proprietary model that incorporated derivative transactions, currency trades and private equity positions. In less than two years, the $15 million became $40 million. The friend of the family used all his influence to enable the wealthy Middle Eastern family to invest an additional $160 million with the investment firm.

A few months later, the president of the investment firm died in a bizarre boating accident off the Cayman Islands. His body was lost at sea. Strangely, the investment firm also vanished with all the money.

The ultra-affluent family retained an accounting firm to find their money. The accounting firm hired a security consulting firm to assist in the process. A lot of the initial efforts consisted of finding where the money initially went and precisely how the proprietary investing model worked. What was uncovered was that no one knew where the money went once it was transferred to a bank in the Cayman Islands. The funds quickly exited the bank, never to be seen again. Furthermore, there was no evidence that any investing was actually done.

With the forensic accountants stymied, the security consulting firm took the lead in the investigation dissecting the lives of all the people involved. The president – a professed only child – turned out to have siblings in France. Talking to them led to a bank in Switzerland which provided leads for the accountants. There were also people in Italy and Greece that needed to be followed up with.

In the meantime, the close friend of the family who made the introduction was being watched and scrutinized. It turned out he received a finder's fee of 20 percent of every investment dollar he brought to the investment firm. This piece of information was never disclosed. This now ex-close friend of the ultra-affluent family in a heart-to-heart conversation with a couple of the niche experts brought in by the security consulting firm chose to return all the monies he received as a finder's fee with interest to the ultra-affluent family.

A year later, the investigators were in the Bahamas where the money and the now — very much alive — president spent a few months. The trail then led to Lichtenstein the home of the Anstalt and to a very dead end.

The security consulting firm continued the search for the president of the investment management firm. Three years from the initial meeting, he was spotted in the very same restaurant where the parties first met. The authorities were brought into the picture and the con artist was arrested.

In the legal negotiations that followed, the ultra-affluent family through the security consultants in conjunction with their lawyers impressed the importance on the con artist of returning the money. He did indeed see the error of his ways and divested himself of about $55 million — all he had left of the $175 million he absconded with.

Asset search and recovery initiatives do not have to necessarily involve globe trotting con artists. Very often they entail finding wealth hidden due to an acrimonious divorce among the rich and powerful. One case involved a husband who, according to his wife, made vanish nearly $8 million in assets owned by his company. While she could not be certain having limited knowledge of the family firm's finances, she was certain a number of company owned properties were not being considered in the proposed divorce settlement.

A detailed examination of the company books did not uncover any malfeasance. However, an intense examination of the husband's life did. He was having an affair with a woman less than half his age who was also an investment banker. By paying very close attention to the business dealings of the girlfriend, the investigators determined that she helped him create an entire shadow corporation, which he owned, that had title to the assets the wife accused him of hiding. As it turned out, $8 million was not at issue, but $14 million.

This same combination of forensic accounting and investigative skills come into play when there are situations where business partners disappear with millions. In one situation, a partner, over a six or seven month time frame, bled his family firm of $12 million dollars. He did this by creating dummy companies that invoiced his family firm which he made sure were paid. With the money in hand, he disappeared leaving his two brothers and sisters with the violated family firm as well as his wife of 24 years and their three children — ages 21, 17 and 14.

It did not take much forensic accounting skill to discern the embezzlement. And, his siblings/partners were initially convinced that there was some egregious mistake in what happened. Moreover, they were also extremely concerned about his well being not believing he would desert them, the family business and especially his wife and children.

A little bit of checking uncovered that he was having an affair for about a year with a 19 year old who worked for him.

When he vanished with the money, she also disappeared. She reappeared in the area six months later after being traded in for a younger model.

It took about a year, following the money trail, until he was found and identified to the police who then arrested him. Along the way we went through about $2 million dollars and at least 12 women. Ten million dollars was recovered. However, in the interim the business failed and the families were torn apart. He is currently serving a 19 year jail sentence.

Another example of asset search and recovery involved the return of six fine art paintings taken from the estate of an affluent client. The combined value of the art was nearly $4 million. In addition two of the pieces had been in the family for three generations. Over a period of two years, all the pieces were recovered. Two pieces were found in the possession of one collector and the remaining four pieces were provided by art brokers of questionable repute who were motivated to help.

Sometimes the client is in line to join the ranks of the financial elite. With the death of the ultra-affluent patriarch, the executor who also happened to be the lawyer who constructed the estate plan as well as drafted the documents went about probating the estate. One of the inheritors concluded that the lawyer was "cheating somehow."

The results of an investigation bore out the inheritor's "hunch." It turned out that the executor created bogus creditors and paid them from the assets in the estate. All told nearly $13 million was paid to these non-existent creditors. Just about all the monies were returned from where they were stashed in offshore accounts.

Litigation support covers an array of investigative initiatives not tied, in the least, to financial dealings. At the extreme there is the ultra-affluent client accused of murder. An extensive investigation was conducted. The result was that the client was shown not to be in the vicinity of the victim at the time of death. Unlike the movies, the real perpetrator of the crime was never identified. Nonetheless, the ultra-affluent client was exonerated which is the primary objective.

Somewhat less dramatic is the case of the affluent client whose intellectual property was purloined. The basis of the defendant's case was that he did not have opportunity and access to the client's intellectual property. After three months, the investigators were able to demonstrate that the defendant did indeed have access and opportunity. The affluent client was awarded damages by the court.

It's increasingly common for security consultants to be called into estate litigation cases. One scenario entailed finding an heir — an illegitimate child. The mirror version, involved demonstrating a self-proclaimed heir was really an imposter. Very often investigative skills coupled with an understanding of the high-net-worth world and estate planning are critical for security consultants in estate litigation cases.

As you can see, there are times security consultants are called in to use their investigative expertise to assist the lawyers make their case on behalf of their wealthy clients. In certain selected situations, security consultants will apply the same investigative expertise to give a business advantage to their high-net-worth clients. This is referred to as competitive intelligence and is also a growing area of the business of the security consultant.

Another area that is seen as going on the offensive is in dealing with abduction cases. Clearly when a high-net-worth client is taken while in another country there is the need to respond through negotiation and sometimes through direct intervention to ensure the safe return of the client. And, there are other times when wealthy clients need to be proactive.

Consider the situation where the child of a wealthy individual is kidnapped by the estranged spouse and illegally brought to another country. Regrettably, this is a growing phenomenon where the hands of the United States government are tied due to national security issues and the like. These crises are probably the most complicated of parental abductions. Just think about the various judicial systems and laws, especially as the kidnapper simply ignores all the custody or restraining orders issued by United States courts.

To successfully recover the child requires an understanding of the relevant laws and regulations where the child has been taken as well as a strong understanding of the country where the recovery will be initiated. It also takes an exceptionally well trained and experienced crisis intervention team to go in and enforce the edicts of the United States courts. Furthermore, it's necessary to have an intimate understanding of the psychological and emotional trauma placed on the child and parent. In the end, a comprehensive team of specialists — attorneys, investigators and other field personnel — are required to recover children abducted by a family member and brought to another country.

All in all, there are times when more forceful interventions are required in order to serve the very legitimate needs of wealthy clients. What is clear is that these times are becoming more numerous. With a greater and growing willingness of criminals to stage more dramatic and intense illegal actions directed at the wealthy, the wealthy are recognizing they have little choice but to push back.

We have provided you with a number of examples of pushing back. While, the intensity of the push back is in part a function of the crisis, it's often more about the willingness and motivations of the wealthy victim. Leading security consultants are exceptionally precise when engaged in this manner. Not only are they attuned to the legal issues, they are equally attuned to the ethical issues. In effect, they know where the line in the sand is drawn and they will not cross it. We strongly advocate that you need to be aware of, and agree with, the moral principles of the security consultant you retain (see **Chapter 5: Caveat Emptor).**

The Limits of the Crisis Intervention Process

The objective of high-quality security consultants when they are called into a crisis situation is to "fix" the problem. As you can imagine, there are multitudinous potential crises that plague the wealthy. Aside from what we have already noted, just consider:

- The yacht hijacked by modern day pirates in the Caribbean. The family kept on board and held for ransom. All the while some of the family members were being serially raped.

- The mistaken kidnapping of the daughter of a very prominent and exceptionally wealthy family who was sold into white slavery and transported to the Far East. (We say "mistaken" because if the slavers knew of her pedigree, they would not have targeted her. Unfortunately, at the time, she was rebelling against her family and "hanging out" with a "fast crowd." Remember, negative migration.)

- The private jet that was repeatedly vandalized. And, on one such occasion, a 12 year old member of the ultra-affluent family which owned the jet was unlucky to be there when the vandals appeared and they crippled him.

- The daughter of a celebrity on the rebound from a particularly bad divorce was "set up" by a potentially very violent criminal. He had provided her with a considerable amount of drugs and had her star in a particularly explicit pornographic movie which was sent to the celebrity. The motivation was extortion.

- The abduction and severe beating of a business owner kidnapped in South America.

The job of your security consultant is to resolve the crisis and provide appropriate ongoing support. With respect to the above situations:

- Facilitate the rescue of the family from the yacht.
- Arrange for the return of the daughter sold into white slavery.
- Ensure that the family's private jet is secure and the family is kept safe.
- Make sure the celebrity's daughter is safe and assist the legal team involved in the case.
- Arrange for the return of the business owner kidnapped in South America.

In situations like these, the wealthy, first and foremost want the crisis contained and resolved. Subsequently, they often require further assistance from arranging psychological counseling to litigation support. Not surprisingly many of the wealthy want vengeance especially in extreme situations like these. They, so badly, want to make the criminals who hurt them and their loved ones "pay."

As we just said, the job of the security consultant is to resolve the crisis and provide appropriate ongoing support. This can very well mean coordinating a team of specially trained rescue operatives to board a yacht and forcibly take command in order to rescue the family from pirates. If in the process, the pirates are hurt, so be it. However, the goal is not to hurt the pirates but to rescue the family and the less conflict the better.

Security consultants are not in the revenge business. They are not out to make the criminals pay, save for providing litigation support. Security consultants are not mercenaries. They are professionals who are called in to remediate BAD situations.

It's far from an anomaly for the wealthy to seek out some sort a tool for vengeance. We sincerely understand their feelings and desires, and do indeed identify with them. However, that is not what high-end security consultants catering to the wealthy do. There is a limit to "going on offense." In selecting a security consultant to intervene in a crisis, you should be cognizant of where they draw the line in the sand.

As we insinuated throughout the book, so much is riding on your choice of a security consultant. So, we now turn to the final chapter of this primer and in many ways the most important chapter — how to find and select a security consultant.

Chapter 5

Caveat Emptor

What would happen if you hired a security consultant bereft of values or scruples?

What would happen if you hired a security consultant who was not aware of the latest innovations in the private client protection field?

What would happen if you hired a security consultant who did not have an in depth understanding of the world of the wealthy and your world in particular?

There are a plethora of people holding themselves out as security consultants. And, most every one of them would be more than happy to work for you. However, few of them are the high-quality professional you really want to work with. In selecting a security consultant there are three rules you need to adhere to. Doing so will result in you achieving your overall goal—being safe and sound.

The security consulting business is big business generating billions of dollars annually. With the increasingly unfriendly world we all live in, the security consulting business is a very solid growth business. From international terrorism to corporate fraud and from homeland security to the recent boom in armed bank robberies, the opportunities for security consulting are expanding nearly exponentially.

At the same time, the corner of the security consulting universe where the clientele are the financial elite generates hundreds of millions of dollars annually. As we can educe from the research findings explained in **Chapter 1: Are You Safe?** and in **Chapter 2: The Protection Concerns of the Wealthy**, the business of protecting the wealthy is also only going to grow. This conclusion has not been lost on the panoply of "authorities" more than eager to do business with you.

As you see the need for such expertise, you face a conundrum. Who do you turn to for security consulting services? Who is going to do the job right? How do you find the "best of the best?"

The Wealthy are Generally Dissatisfied with Their Security Consultants

The experience of many high-net-worth individuals with security consultants has been less than exceptional. First, the majority of high-net-worth people in our national study (75.4%) have employed the services of a security consultant within the last three years (Exhibit 5.1). Here we're using the term security consultant to cover anyone providing any type of security solution from those that take a holistic approach to security consultants who limit their services to upgrading house alarm systems. Every one of the ultra-affluent save for one person (98.7%), four out of five of the affluent (80.3%) as well as a smaller but significant proportion (63.1%) of the low-end affluent hired some kind of security consultant during this time frame.

Exhibit 5.1: Employed a Security Consultant Within the Last 3 Years

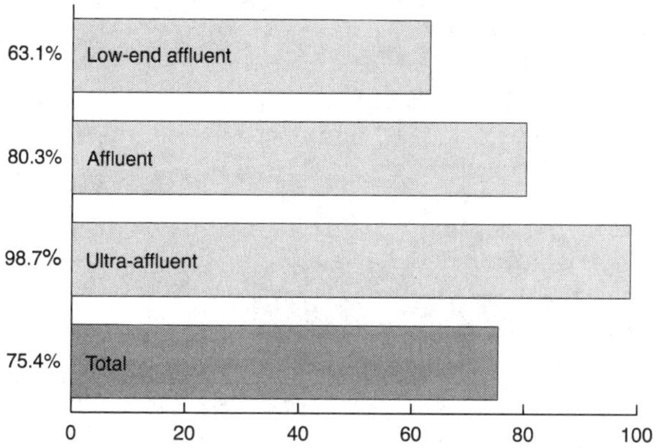

N = 427 Wealthy Individuals

Were there was more than one security consulting firm employed, we're focusing on the security consulting firm that was given the largest monetary contract. Of the 322 wealthy individuals who employed the services of a security consultant within the last three years, less than half of them (45.7%) were highly satisfied with the quality of service they received (Exhibit 5.2). More informative is that as the levels of wealth increase, there is a statistical difference in the percentage of wealthy individuals who are highly satisfied. In other words, the more affluent are proportionately less satisfied.

Exhibit 5.2: Highly Satisfied with the Level of Service Received

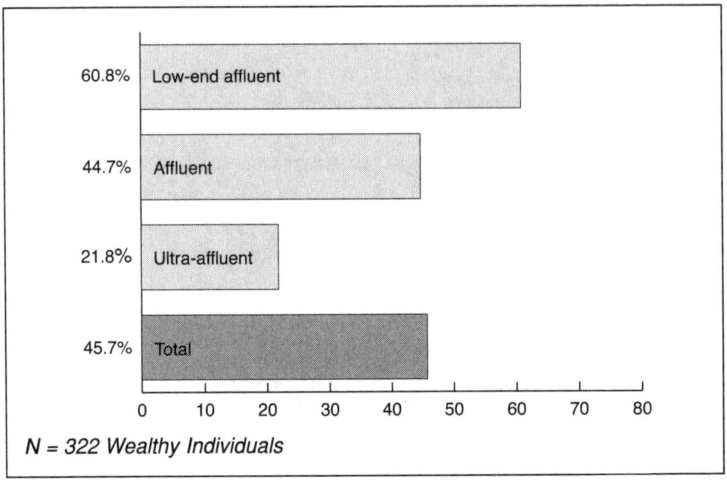

Not being highly satisfied with the service performed by the security consultant is not necessarily indicative that he or she was not doing a good job. Still, only 28.6 percent reported that they believed the quality of the work done by their security consultant was superior (Exhibit 5.3). The pattern among the various levels of wealth on this issue mirrors the response pattern on the matter of high satisfaction. In effect, the greater the affluence the less likely the security consultant was seen as doing a superior job.

Exhibit 5.3: Thought the Job the Security Consultant did was Superior

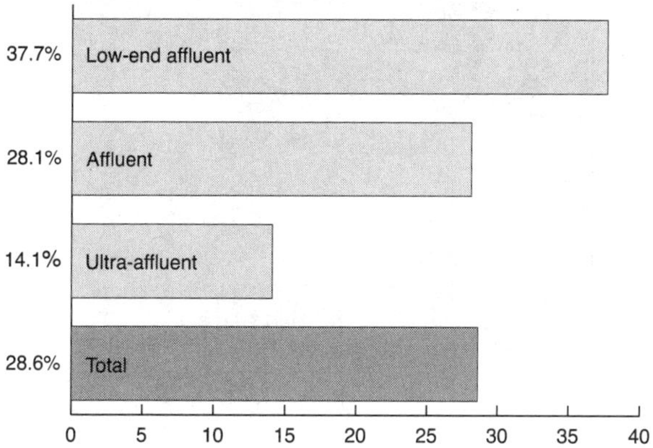

N = 322 Wealthy Individuals

What proves to be more instructive is the willingness of high-net-worth clients to (1) employ the security consultant again and (2) recommend him or her to other people. If a wealthy client would, when appropriate, rehire their security consultant as well as refer the professional to their peers and business associates, then we can say the security consultant did an excellent job.

As we can see in Exhibit 5.4, only 26.4 percent of the 322 wealthy individuals who had hired a security consultant would indeed use that same person another time when similar needs arose. Once again, we observe the pattern where greater wealth being more critical and possibly more demanding is consequently less inclined to employ the same security consultants for the same services once more.

Exhibit 5.4: Would Employ the Security Consultant Again

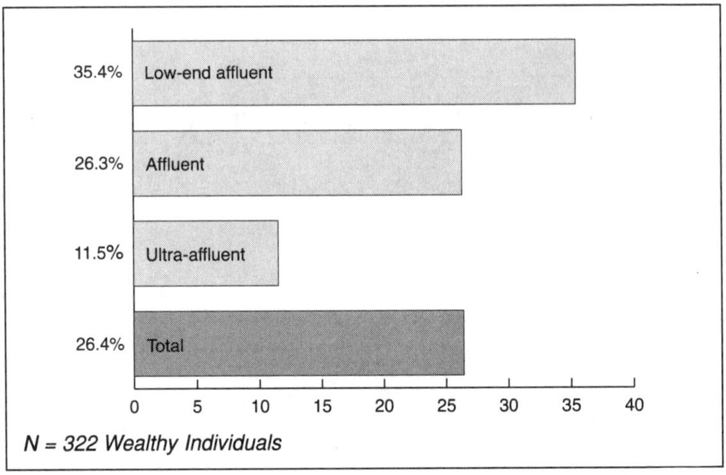

Not only will proportionately very few high-net-worth clients do repeat business with their security consultants, a slightly smaller percentage (23.6%) would refer these security consultants to a peer or business associate (Exhibit 5.5). The same trend of greater affluence being a poorer referral source for the security consultant is in evidence.

Exhibit 5.5: Would Recommend the Security Consultant to Others

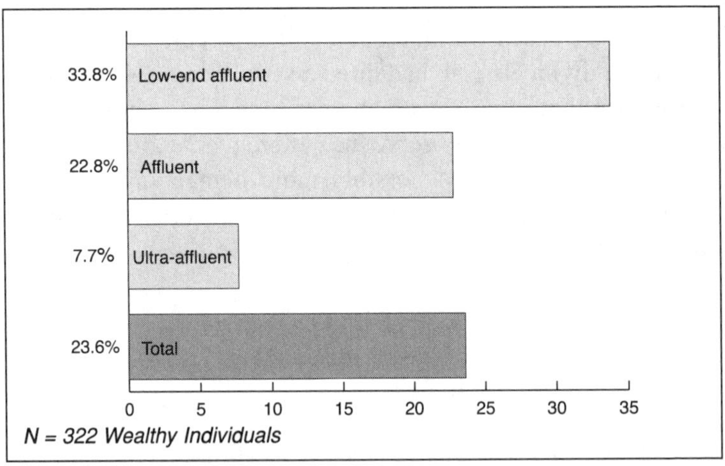

In research study after research study of purchasers of professional services—especially among the wealthy—we observe that there is a greater perceived risk of making a "bad referral" to a peer or business associate than re-employing a service provider. And, this behavioral pattern is also in evidence when it comes to security consulting. So it comes as no big surprise that a smaller percentage of the wealthy who have employed the services of security consultants would refer them to others than re-hire them when the situation demands.

What does this component of the national study of the wealthy tell us? We can conclude from these results that the wealthy do indeed avail themselves of security consultants which is not surprising considering their overall perspectives (see **Chapter 1: Are You Safe?**) as well as their protection concerns (see **Chapter 2: Protection Concerns of the Wealthy**). We can also conclude that, in general, the quality of the security consulting services they are receiving is not up to the standards they are expecting.

When it comes to crafting and implementing security solutions for the financial elite, there should not be any question of the quality of the service. It must be exceptional. While this should be the case with all clients, considering that the wealthy are specifically purchasing premier services, they should be receiving premier services.

That said, the question is: "Why are the wealthy not getting superior security consulting services?" While there is always the possibility of a glitch, the predominant rationale for the paucity of wealthy individuals being highly satisfied and consistently receiving superior service is that they did a less than exemplary job of finding, selecting and working with a security consultant.

Always remember, it's your "world" that you're responsible for protecting. It takes a concerted effort and knowledge to find a top-flight security consultant you can work well with. The effort is all you, while in the rest of the chapter we detail the knowledge you will need.

Finding Your Security Consultant

There are a variety of ways the wealthy locate all sorts of professionals with whom they then do business. Whether it's for legal services or medical services or financial services, the optimal means of finding a top-flight professional is through referrals. Someone whose judgment you trust provides you with an introduction to the type of professional you're seeking.

The very same logic holds for the security consulting services for the wealthy we have discussed herein. The nature of all high-end services makes referrals a risk mitigation strategy in selecting a provider. Specifically, we're referring to:

- The intangibility of the offering.
- The perceived complexity of the offering.
- The desire on your part to work with "authorities" coupled with a general inability to identify the "authorities."

Intangibility. For most of the wealthy, security services are something of a mystery. Many of the services a security consultant provides can rarely be seen or touched or evaluated directly. There is no way you can do the side-to-side comparison as you might for a stereo system, or road test these services as you would when buying a new car. Thus it's wise to turn to referrals from people whose judgment you trust.

Complexity. Your protection concerns are important, unique and complicated. Consequently, you will need to find a security consultant who can address the variety of security related situations and issues you face. While many security consultants can talk a good game, few can deliver holistically; few can effectively meet the security needs of the wealthy. If you want someone who can efficaciously deal with the complexity and particularities of the financial elite, you will need to get a referral to a security professional with a proven track record in this regard.

Reliance on "authorities." We have yet to meet a high-net-worth individual who did not want to work with an expert —a true authority on crafting security solutions for the wealthy. Using the medical analogy again, if you have a serious medical problem, do you not want the expert specialist to be your doctor, or will the local general practitioner be sufficient? Of course, you would opt for the expert medical specialist. The best way to find out if a security consultant is an authority on dealing with the unique protection needs of the wealthy is to get the opinions of other wealthy people or other authorities. What we see is that the significantly well-to-do generally turn to people whose opinions they give considerable credence when it comes to selecting high-end professional services.

The Wealthy Turn to Their Professional Advisors

Nearly all of our high-net-worth clients come to us through referrals. Every once in a while we're introduced to new clients from current clients, but most often we're called in by professional advisors to address the protection needs of their wealthy clients. This is the norm for all security consultants catering to the financial elite.

More than ever leading private client lawyers as well as accountants catering to the wealthy are bringing security consultants to the table. In ever greater numbers, security consultants are also receiving numerous calls from family office executives who are learning about them from their ultra-affluent clients or from the aforementioned professionals as well as private bankers and investment managers whose clientele is also the financial elite.

In order to be responsive to their high-net-worth clients, these professional advisors are increasingly providing guidance with respect to managing the risks associated with their protection concerns. Hence, they are actively seeking out and vetting security consultants. Moreover, these professionals are making attending to their high-net-worth clients' security concerns part of a broader service offering. They are appropriately taking on the responsibility of coordinating and overseeing a number of ongoing critical issues facing the wealthy with personal security being one of these critical issues. Just consider the following examples of professionals bringing in security consultants.

A law firm with a private client unit catering to perpetual tourists. Also known as "permanent travelers" or "nomadic millionaires" or "golden ghosts," the world of the perpetual tourist is esoteric even by the standards of the ultra-affluent. These wealthy individuals are the ultimate in leveraging the rules of sovereignty for their financial benefit. While they have citizenship (sometimes multiple citizenships), they never officially reside in one location long enough to pay taxes there. They will even sometimes advantage themselves of the nation states who use their nationality for fundraising.

This roaming lifestyle often coupled with a need for opacity results in numerous security concerns. With a tremendous reliance on communication technology there are often extensive gaps in the security of their communications. With property situated in different locations across the world, there is usually a strong need for state-of-the-art residential security systems and, more importantly, repeated vetting of personnel with access to these properties. Close protection tends to be required on an as needed basis predicated on the location and agenda of the ultra-affluent client. Continuous monitoring of their identities is a must as are crisis contingency plans.

While the law firm deals with the matter of asset protection planning, for various other protection needs, their clientele looks to them to supervise their delivery—a role they have purposefully taken on. The law firm identified and vetted the security consulting firms it recommends to its clientele. Furthermore, the law firm directly oversees the relationship between the security consulting firm and its wealthy clients.

The family office. The concept of the family office probably originated at the end of the 17th century and into the beginning of the 18th century with the Rothschild family. With slow growth until the 1980s, the family office concept has recently taken off. There are an estimated 3,000 to 4,000 family offices throughout the United States and a somewhat fewer number throughout the rest of the world.

The family office acts as the financial center for a wealthy family. Its objective is to preserve and enhance the wealth of the family. By pooling the assets of the family, the family office is positioned to garner economies of scale, the ability to benefit from the latest tax strategies geared to the ultra-affluent, create anonymity for family members, deal with an array of administrative matters (e.g., bill paying) and maximize philanthropic endeavors. At their core, however, family offices are mostly about investing a very significant amount of money.

Today, there are a number of different versions of the family office. The single family office generally caters to a single family that often has aggregate wealth in excess of $100 million. The multiple family office tend to serve between 5 and 20 ultra-affluent families. Due to the nature and orientation of the family office, there are a wide variety of protection issues that arise.

A growing trend is for the family office to help make sure the family is safe and sound. One family office after arranging for a security audit on its own operation as well as the security of key family members recognized the need to make dramatic changes. For the family office, the need to take steps to ensure privacy included actions as simple as shredding all documents before they are thrown away and education on how not to give away passwords to electronic countermeasures and the use of encryption software.

For the family, a number of security solutions were implemented. Educational programs for family members concerning how, as one family member put it, "not be stupid." Extensive background checks on all the people intersecting their lives uncovered a number of employees who lied to get their jobs and were let go. Transporter services were used for critical documents and property and occasionally family members. And, extensive crisis contingency plans were implemented if something was to go wrong.

As with many law firms, family offices that are bringing security consultants into the picture are taking an oversight role. The executives of the family office are acting as monitors and evaluators of the security consultants.

Business management firms. Celebrity entertainers and athletes religiously rely on a number of professional advisors to shape their careers and manage their financial lives. Business managers are unfailingly one of those professional advisors catering to a celebrity's financial concerns and preferences.

Business managers often deal with the array of financial issues impacting the lives of their famous wealthy clients. Included here are bill paying, overseeing investments and scrutinizing tax strategies. In quite a number of instances, business managers also—through proxies—pick up the laundry, make sure the dog is taken to the veterinarian and even make sure birthday cards are sent to important relatives. In sum, many business managers play a central role in the lives of their well-healed celebrity clients.

As we have seen in a number of examples, one of the problems celebrities confront is an extreme loss of privacy. From the paparazzi to fans to stalkers, the life of a celebrity is sometimes lived in a fishbowl. To deal with this issue among its clientele security consulting firms are, more than ever, engaged by business management firms on behalf of their famous clients.

For selected celebrities and their families, the security consulting firm creates, to varying degrees, a zone of privacy and protection around them. The security solutions range from electronic countermeasures (more than one listening devise was found in the homes of celebrities), to personnel transporter services, to extensive close protection. Expertise such as forensic document analysis to evaluate the love letters as well as the threats, state-of-the-art security systems at residences, disinformation initiatives directed at the paparazzi including the use of body doubles and continuous re-screening of personal assistants and other employees can become business as usual.

To better serve their wealthy clients, what we're seeing throughout the private client protection industry is that professional advisors are increasingly taking the lead in indirectly providing security solutions to the wealthy. Many of these professional advisors are adept at one set of security solutions — asset protection planning. Hence, they are taking on the apposite coordinator role when it comes to all the other potential security solutions.

What does this mean to you? Bottom line: ask around. In today's world, the professional advisors you turn to — in particular your attorneys, accountants, bankers and money managers — should be able to point you in the right direction.

While these professionals will be able to introduce you to security consultants and while many of them will provide critical oversight functions, you must still control the selection process. To this end there are a number of guidelines you should adhere to in making your selection of a security consultant.

Selecting a Security Consultant

It's often quite difficult to evaluate professionals like security consultants when they are providing their services because of their intangibility (see above). Moreover, the very nature of the field defines success in the negative. That is, when nothing happens (e.g., a kidnapping or a burglary does not occur) then, *ipso facto*, a good job is being done. Consequently, you have to trust the judgment and expertise of your security consultant although your active involvement (see below) provides you a window to see what is going on and make better decisions—including the decision as to whom to work with.

Even though you must trust the security consultant, that does not mean you should select one without careful screening. It's your responsibility to exercise due diligence when you choose a security consultant. There are three guidelines you need to follow when choosing a security consultant. They are:

- Guideline #1: Choose a security consultant with integrity.

- Guideline #2: Choose a security consultant who is a technical expert.

- Guideline #3: Choose a security consultant with experience working with the wealthy.

By closely following these guidelines, you will be able to avoid all the many less than qualified self-proclaimed authorities who will be delighted to take your money without delivering value in return. It's important that you maintain perspective. These guidelines are not absolutes. Instead, they are geared to ensure you're making a wise decision when it comes to choosing a security consultant to work with.

Keep in mind that anyone—anyone at all—can call themselves a security consultant. There are no restrictions on using the title. Within the universe of private client security consulting, one of the most noteworthy examples of a dubious security consultant was the now defunct firm of Almos Mine Executive Services.

With impeccable credentials the partners of Almos Mine Executive Services would sell their security consulting expertise to high-net-worth individuals and corporations. Unfortunately, there were a number of incidents where their expertise fell short as their clients were robbed of valuables such as paintings and jewelry in the case of the wealthy and intellectual property and money (i.e., embezzlement) in the case of corporate clients.

After a run of nearly ten years, the partners of Almos Mine Executive Services got sloppy which was, no doubt, a function of hubris–as evidenced in the naming of their security consulting firm. In a string of missteps, indicative of the Keystone Cops, they were caught in the act of stealing from their clients. While this is an extreme example of what can happen if you select the "wrong" security consultant, it's a cautionary tale that you need to remember.

One protection concern of the wealthy that has been ripe for shysters is asset protection planning. The more blatant examples include promoters hawking offshore solutions such as "unbreakable secret trusts" and "your own bank" to the marketing of pure trusts otherwise known as patriot trusts, contract trusts, final trusts, foreign common law trust organizations and complex trust systems.

If you have not yet been pitched a pure trust in one of its many incarnations, it's often part of a three-tiered trust structure. The objective is to veil the existence of the trust while making the structure tax free. In the real world, nothing is accomplished except to attract the attention of the Internal Revenue Service.

Even among well intentioned security consultants there is a clear hierarchy of talent and capabilities. The same is the case among professionals who specialize in asset protection planning, for instance. In a study sponsored by Trusts & Estates magazine, we were able to discern that only a small percentage of private client lawyers who identified themselves as being specialists at asset protection planning were indeed knowledgeable concerning many of the asset protection strategies that the wealthy can, very legitimately, bring to bear.

We found that there is a significant gap between private client lawyers' current competency levels and their ideal skill levels (Exhibit 5.6). Only 16.3 percent of the lawyers surveyed currently rate themselves as an authority on asset protection strategies and techniques even though they readily position themselves as asset protection specialists. There are other indications of a low level of expertise. Just 13.2 percent of private client lawyers say they are very familiar with the Uniform Fraudulent Transfer Act. Moreover, private client lawyers agree that there is an expertise gap. Overall, 73.6 percent agree that they need to become more knowledgeable about asset protection strategies and techniques.

Exhibit 5.6: Delivering Asset Protection Expertise

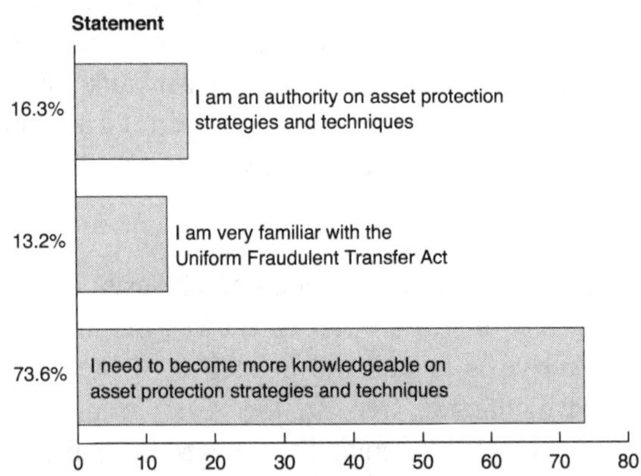

N = 227 self-identified asset protection lawyers

Another indication that many private client lawyers need to enhance their asset protection expertise is that a meaningful number of them are unfamiliar with some of the strategies and techniques in the field (Exhibit 5.7). While most are comfortable with such strategies such as corporate structures, outright gifts to family members and limited liability companies, far fewer felt they were experts in areas such as offshore self-settled trusts, life insurance and equity stripping.

Exhibit 5.7: Familiar with Specific Asset Protection Strategies and Techniques

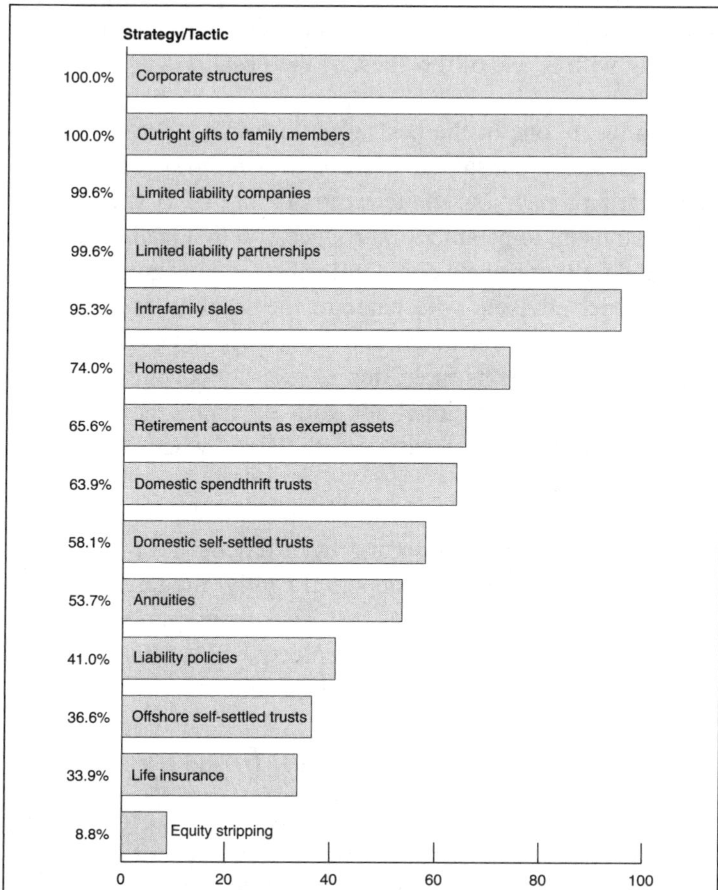

N = 227 self-identified asset protection lawyers

This survey indicates that significant percentages of private client lawyers do not feel completely prepared to offer asset protection planning at the level of professionalism appropriate to the wealthy. These private client lawyers feel they need more expertise in the area in order to deliver the quality of service they are accustomed to giving.

Never forget that we're talking about your personal well being, the well being of the people you care about, your confidential information, your wealth and your property. Consequently, it's your responsibility — your obligation to yourself and others — to make sure that the person you're working with is one of the "best of the best."

To recap, one of the best ways to find a potentially high-quality security consultant is through a referral. The referral can be from a peer, but the tendency is for one of your professional advisors to be able to introduce you to a leading authority in the field of private client protection. Let us not forget that professional advisors who cater to the wealthy and who are truly attentive to their needs and wants will have a number of high-net-worth clients interested in security consulting services. Thus, these professional advisors are doing their due diligence separating the wheat from the chaff when it comes to security consultants.

While the introduction and even having the professional advisor provide oversight can significantly mitigate the possibility of hiring the wrong security consultant, you should still be involved in making the final selection. Therefore, we will now go more in depth on the three guidelines.

Guideline #1: Proven Integrity

Integrity is first and foremost in importance. The veracity of your security consultant is a must. Just as people trust your judgment, there are many times you will have to trust the judgment of your security consultants. More specifically, there may be times when you will have to trust their judgment without being privy to their rationale. Hence, you need to take the necessary actions to determine whether you're, in fact dealing with an ethical security consultant. There are three things you absolutely must do:

- *Make sure they are endorsed by people you trust.* It's like any other professional you would hire; you're looking for someone who has worked with someone whose considered opinion you trust. As noted above, the best referral source is usually a professional advisor such as your accountant or attorney, but it could easily be another person in a similar socio-economic and lifestyle position.

- *Know where they draw the line in the sand.* It's extremely important that you know what your security consultant will and will not do. This would become apparent as you work with him or her, however by defining the parameters up front you will get a good picture of the moral grounding of the person you're dealing with.

- *Understand the conditions under which they will fire a high-net-worth client.* Periodically, leading security consultants will fire one of their wealthy clients. Generally speaking, when wealthy clients choose not to adhere to advice the security consultant provides and by doing so, they are not only endangering themselves but the security consultant, it's time for them to find a new security consultant.

Guideline #2: Extensive Technical Expertise

Of course, no one person can be adept at all aspects and variations of providing security solutions for the financial elite. Instead, what you want is:

- A security consultant that works with you through a process that determines what you need to do.

- A security consultant who can access niche experts to deliver selected specialty security solutions.

- A security consultant with the expertise and sensitivity to act as coordinator and overseer of any security solution implemented.

- A security consultant who can create a gestalt of all the various appropriate security solutions you require.

- A security specialist who is at the cutting edge of the private client protection industry.

Your security consultant should have a broad understanding of the different protection concerns and appropriate security solutions as well as a comprehensive understanding of selected areas. Hence, the security consultant you want to work with will have a broad knowledge of the four sets of protection concerns discussed in this book and what actions can be taken to deal with these concerns and who are especially proficient—the niche experts—in providing the appropriate security solutions.

There are a number of guide posts that will be telling if your security consultants are technically adept. When they are endorsed by someone such as your attorney, your lawyer is not only vouching for their integrity, he or she is also standing up for them as a technical expert based on the due diligence they conducted.

Their background is another guide post. You want to know their career history as security consultants. Included here is being recognized in the industry as an expert is probably one of the better demonstrations of a truly capable security consultant. Published works, speaking engagements and the like are signs that others recognize the technical expertise of the security consultant.

Guideline #3: Experience Working with the Wealthy

The backgrounds, the stresses and the lifestyles of the affluent, especially the ultra-affluent, are truly inimitable. The world of the wealthy is very different, to say the least, from those of less wealth as well as the corporate environment. It's therefore wise to work with high-quality security consultants who are attuned to your world—the world of wealth.

It's not uncommon to see security consultants who are quite adept in the corporate world failing to live up to their promise when they make the transition to the world of the wealthy. The characteristics of the corporate client compared to the wealthy client can be, and faithfully are, significantly different. So much so that it's common for corporate security consultants after making the transition to be ineffectual if not dangerous to their affluent clients.

All the research and training about the idiosyncrasies of the various security solutions cannot possibly take the place of the insights gained from experience in working with the wealthy. These insights prove crucial when it comes to successful implementation.

Taking this one step further, the security consultant you want to work with spends the time to really understand what you want to accomplish, what you need to accomplish and all you doubts and anxieties, and then is always thinking of ways to be responsive to you. Your security consultant should always be considering your unique situation and ways to improve things for you. Here, your security consultant is moving from the generic world of the wealthy to your distinct situation.

How to Work with Your Security Consultant

It's not enough to select a good, let alone great, security consultant. You also have to work with your choice. You have to be involved. It's akin to a good marriage; it works because both parties work at it.

As we noted, education is center stage in order to ensure you and your family as well as your possessions are safe and sound—which is the rationale for this book. Your security consultant, therefore, should be an educator. Knowledge transferred from your security consultant to you and others is a requisite.

Why would top-of-the-line security consultants share so much with you? Would doing so diminish their value and thus their ability to make a living? On the contrary, knowledge transfer results in you having a better understanding of the value you're getting for your money. At the same time, in the private client protection industry, there is usually a big gap between education and making it happen – between knowing and doing. You might know what it takes to avoid a three-point surveillance team, but does that mean you can?

Working with a high-quality security consultant is an education. At the end, you should not expect to become a security consultant to the wealthy, but you should understand why particular security solutions are the optimal ones for you – all things considered.

Knowledge transfer, at the level we're discussing, is instrumental. The result is an avoidance of miscommunications. The following can therefore be of assistance:

Have your security consultant explain how the processes they are using work. Leading security consultants focus on processes. Here we discussed the Protection Planning Process and the Crisis Intervention Process. While different security consultants might have their own variations, basically if they fail to approach the matter in this regard, they are doing you a disservice.

Have your security consultant explain the alternative ways of achieving and managing your protection concern. In **Chapter 3: The Protection Planning Process** we discussed two conceptual algorithms: the "need for a security solution" and the "net value of a security solution." Make sure you understand the various security solutions in the context of these conceptual algorithms.

Have your security consultant explain, in detail, how each selected security solution operates. By having such an understanding the viability of the selected security solution is greatest. Moreover, this way you will also clearly know the limitations of the selected security solutions you have chosen.

Have you security consultant explain how all the security solutions you're considering impact your various protection concerns. The various security solutions impact different protection needs to various degrees. It's important that you clearly understand how taking certain actions will benefit you in other ways.

When it comes to greater affluence and larger families, we find that a champion is needed in order to ensure that the wealthy family's protection needs are effectively addressed. The champion is a conduit between the family members and the security consultant. Many times this role is provided by a professional advisor such as the wealthy family's attorney. Sometimes it's a family member. More and more, as in the case of family offices, a senior staff member of the family office assumes the role. Family member or professional advisor, the champion is close to the family, has a keen understanding of the family dynamics and is capable and trusted to make major decisions in the event of a crisis.

A Personal Note

In our experience we find a fair number of high-net-worth individuals who would rather just turn over the reins to a security consultant. We strongly believe that to do the best job for our clients we need their involvement. The clients we prefer to work with are the ones who are intelligent and informed.

We have found our clients to be quite intelligent. Very few people of significant wealth attained their largess by being stupid. And, we avoid stupid people. These people prove to be a detriment to themselves as well as to us. We're very willing to fire high-net-worth clients who act in ways that are inclined to create severe security problems.

As noted, we strongly believe in knowledge transfer. This enables our high-net-worth clients to make well informed decisions. We employ the proven processes discussed herein as the framework to not only surface what needs to be done but as a pedagogical tool resulting in well educated clients. By working hard to educate intelligent clients, in the end, everyone is very satisfied and, most importantly, our high-net-worth clients are safe and sound.

Are You Safe Yet?

Quotidian acts of evil are perpetrated against people with the more affluent among us certainly a prime target. With the world replete with very real threats to your well being and the safety of those people and things of import, and after going through the Protection Planning Process; after all this focused effort: "Are you safe yet?"

Regretfully, the answer has not changed: "Maybe." In the final analysis, there is absolutely no way to assure that a determined criminal will not kidnap your children, will not steal your identity, will not steal your wealth or will not burglarize your home. Sadly, no matter how many precautions you take, no matter how diligent you are there is no way to **one hundred percent guarantee** your security, the security of your loved ones, the security of your confidential information, the security of your wealth or the security of your property. As we noted in **Chapter 1: Are You Safe?** bulletproof security is not an option.

That is the glass is half empty view. Now, let us consider the matter the other way around. After all this focused effort: "Are you safe yet?" You and your loved ones, your confidential information, your wealth and your belongings are probably exponentially safer now than ever before.

Presuming you will not adopt the security solution of Howard Hughes and sequester yourself and your loved ones in some sort of fortress, then by going through the Protection Planning Process and implementing the appropriate security solutions, you're doing what is reasonable and wise. Keep in mind that a core attribute of this approach is your extensive involvement. Thus, your security solutions are customized to your world. Moreover, by being in the driver's seat, by being educated on the various options, you have made *intelligent* and *informed* decisions.

Returning to the "mirror test," you can look in the mirror and say you're taking all reasonable and meaningful steps to protect all that is important to you. By understanding the risks and implementing customized security solutions, you're taking a very low probability and mitigating it. Although anything can happen, you have passed the "mirror test."

Appendix A

Analytic Modeling Methodology

In Chapter 1: Are Your Safe? we centered our perspective on the affluent. We discussed the analytic model we employed to size this universe. The findings on the affluent are based on the private wealth industry's single largest and most diverse database of the affluent. We have systematically collected broad-spectrum data on the affluent, our data covering the wealthy who work with all institutions and all types of financial advisors, including brokers, private bankers, registered investment advisors, financial planners, life insurance professionals, bankers, accountants, attorneys, family offices and, of course, security specialists.

Although the databases employed were culled for empirically derived insights into the affluent, some limitations due to sample size across studies existed, even using meta-analytic approaches. We therefore combined our empirical research findings with the perceptions and interpretations of leading professional advisors.

With respect to the analytic modeling, we used this approach because analytic modeling is one of several methodologies to size or estimate what cannot be measured directly and it's the preferred approach for assessing a market such as the affluent. Because the methodology we utilized is but one way of generating estimates, however, we validated its results against other modeling techniques.

At its core, analytic modeling uses a multi-equation approach to create scenarios or best-estimates of the current size of the affluent universe across predetermined, asset-sized segments. In this case, the analytic model was constructed of a series of equations resulting in deterministic algorithms. The data the model was built on focus on a variety of issues such as the impact of tax policies on the behavior of the affluent, as well as the calculations of other analysts.

In order to create the analytic model, 27,904 data points were used. Each data point "footed" to two or more primary and/or secondary sources. These data points were obtained from 133 different sources such as think tanks, financial institutions, industry consultants, academicians, and governmental organizations. The sources included:

- Merrill Lynch
- The Spectrem Group
- The Global Policy Forum
- New York University
- The Lazard Trust
- The World Bank
- Cornell University
- The Essenes Trust
- FinCEN
- The Institute for Intergovernmental Research
- The Soloton Society
- The International Association for Research in Income and Wealth

A critical issue in the process was to ensure we excluded any "tainted money" in the model. Thus, wherever there was a meaningful chance (i.e., a 10 percent or greater probability that the private wealth in question is a function of illegal activities as defined by the United States going back two generations) the wealth is "tainted money," we excluded it from the model.

There are two areas to closely examine when evaluating the output of an analytic model such as this. The first is the quality of the data incorporated into the model. The old saw is "garbage in, garbage out" meaning that a model is only as good as the data upon which it's based. As noted, we address this threat to validity by closely examining each data point, requiring multiple confirmations before including it in the model. In effect, every data point was checked and double-checked, and when questions were raised and estimates were required, specific content matter experts were called in.

The other potential threat to validity is assumptions made about how core measures interact because a change in structural relationships can have a cascade effect on the calculations. We approached this issue by creating scenarios where the core measures were systematically manipulated. During this process, we conducted sensitivity analyses to provide a better understanding of the likelihood of each conclusion.

As anyone who has done modeling knows, these calculations are a function of the quality of the data introduced into the analytic model. Obviously, changes in these numbers will alter the conclusions, which is why we undertook so much model testing and paid so much attention to issues of reliability and validity.

Appendix B

Sampling Methodology

The approach detailed in this book is predicated on the explicit and implicit needs, wants, protection concerns, anxieties and relevant experience of the wealthy. We derive much of our understanding of these issues empirically and we then augment these research derived insights with our extensive experience "in the trenches." Here we want to put in perspective the nature of the empirical work we do by discussing the sampling methodology we employ.

In studying the wealthy, we do not engage in probability sampling. Quite the opposite, we employ a nonprobability sampling process commonly referred to as snowball sampling. The difference between nonprobability and probability sampling is that nonprobability sampling does not involve random selection and probability sampling does. This does not mean that nonprobability samples are not representative of the population, but it does mean that nonprobability samples cannot depend upon the rationale of probability theory.

With a probabilistic sample, the odds or probability that the population is represented can be computed; the confidence intervals for the statistics can be estimated. With nonprobability samples, there is a risk that the population is not estimated well, although there are statistical controls that are applied. When possible, probabilistic or random sampling methods are preferred over nonprobabilistic ones. However, it's accepted practice in applied social science research to employ nonprobability sampling approaches in circumstances where it's not feasible, practical or theoretically sensible to do random sampling.

Broadly, nonprobability sampling methods can be divided into two broad types: accidental or purposive. Snowball sampling, like most sampling methods, is purposive in nature because the sampling problem is usually approached with a specific plan in mind. In nonprobability purposive sampling, sampling is performed with one or more specific predefined groups in mind, such as the wealthy.

Purposive sampling is very useful for situations where a targeted sample cannot be cost-efficiently reached using probability methods. The risk of nonprobability purposive sampling is that subgroups in the target population that are more readily accessible may be overweighted. Nonprobability purposive sampling approaches include modal instance sampling, expert sampling, quota sampling and heterogeneity sampling, as well as snowball sampling.

One important caveat when surveying the wealthy is they must be compensated for their time. As a participant in this study, each wealthy individual was given a $500 honorarium. Moreover, each wealthy individual was surveyed in person by a trained interviewer.

Appendix C

High-net-worth Sample Demographics

In order to better understand their protection needs and concerns we conducted a national survey of the wealthy. Demographics are characteristics that can be used to describe a sample. The four demographic factors considered here are:

- Amount of wealth.
- Age.
- Gender
- Source of wealth.

The demographics of the sample are very much in line with previous research of the wealthy. This indicates the representativeness of the sample.

Amount of Wealth

In considering the affluent, we divided the sample into the low-end affluent (those individuals with net-worths between $1 million and $5 million), the affluent (those individuals with net-worths between $5 million and $25 million) and the ultra-affluent (those individuals with net-worths of $25 million or more) (see **Chapter 1: Are You Safe?** for a discussion of the varieties of affluence).

In our research, the low-end affluent comprised 48.2 percent of the sample, the affluent comprised 33.3 percent of the sample with the ultra-affluent comprising the remaining 18.5 percent (Exhibit C.1).

Exhibit C.1: Amount of Wealth

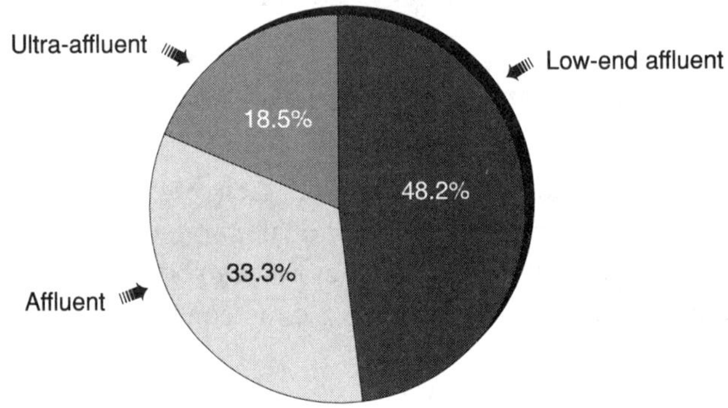

N = 427 Wealthy Individuals

Age

The majority of the sample (59.7%) was 50 years old or greater (Exhibit C.2). As the level of affluence increases, the proportion of the wealthy individuals 50 years old or greater increases to where those 50 years old or more represent 86.1 percent of the ultra-affluent.

Exhibit C.2: Age

Age	Low-end affluent	Affluent	Ultra-Affluent	Total
<50 years old	55.8%	32.4%	13.9%	40.3%
50 years old or more	44.2%	67.6%	86.1%	59.7%

N = 427 Wealthy Individuals

Gender

Men were the primary decision makers in the sample (Exhibit C.3). Overall, 70.3 percent of the respondents were male. As with age, as the level of affluence increases, the proportion of the segments that are male increases from 57.8 percent for the low-end affluent to 76.8 percent for the affluent and 91.1 percent for the ultra-affluent.

Exhibit C.3: Gender

Gender	Low-end affluent	Affluent	Ultra-Affluent	Total
Male	57.8%	76.8%	91.1%	70.3%
Female	42.2%	23.2%	8.9%	29.7%

N = 427 Wealthy Individuals

Source of Wealth

We repeatedly find in study after study that privately held businesses (including the sale of privately held businesses) are the principle legitimate way of amassing significant wealth. Such is also the case in this program of research.

A strong majority (64.2%) of the respondents became wealthy through equity in a privately held business (Exhibit C.4). Nearly all the ultra-affluent (97.5%) generated their fortunes this way whereas 66.9 percent of the affluent did so and 49.5 percent of the low-end affluent did so. There are a number of ways of becoming wealthy such as corporate employment, inheritance and investments. Nevertheless, the principle way of obtaining extreme wealth is nearly always tied to a very successful privately held company. Even celebrities that command multi-million dollar pay checks regularly invest those monies in business ventures that translate into greater wealth than their considerable paychecks.

Exhibit C.4: Source of Wealth

Source of Wealth	Low-end affluent	Affluent	Ultra-Affluent	Total
Privately held firm	49.5%	66.9%	97.5%	64.2%
Other	50.5%	33.1%	2.5%	35.8%

N = 427 Wealthy Individuals